THE ARCHITECTURE I
LONDON

For Jim, Zoe & Erin

THE ARCHITECTURE LOVER'S GUIDE TO
LONDON

SIAN LYE

WHITE OWL

AN IMPRINT OF PEN & SWORD BOOKS LTD.
YORKSHIRE – PHILADELPHIA

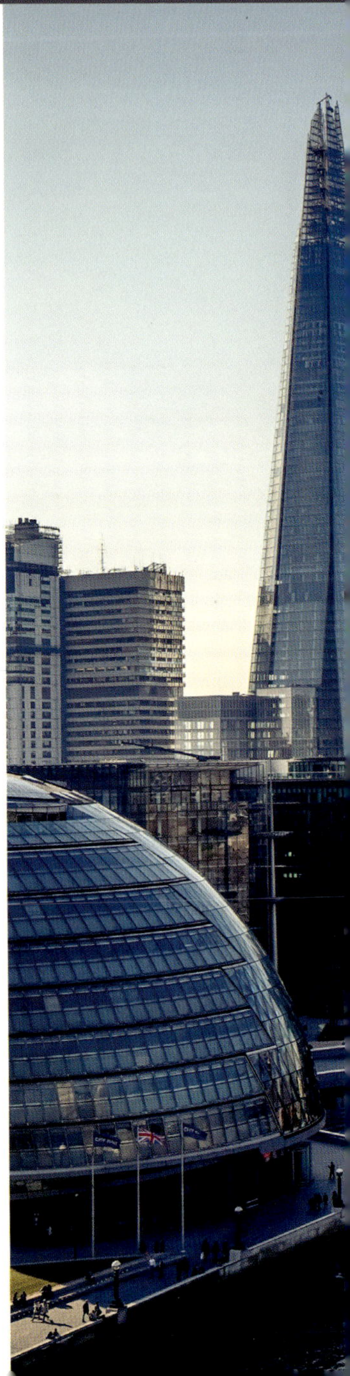

First published in Great Britain in 2022 by
White Owl
An imprint of
Pen & Sword Books Ltd
Yorkshire - Philadelphia

ISBN 978 1 39900 166 3

All photographs Adobe Stock apart from where otherwise
indicated.

A CIP catalogue record for this book is available from the
British Library.

Printed and bound by Short Run Press Limited, Exeter, England.
Design: SJmagic DESIGN SERVICES, India.

Pen & Sword Books Ltd incorporates the imprints of
Pen & Sword Books Archaeology, Atlas, Aviation, Battleground,
Discovery, Family History, History, Maritime, Military, Naval,
Politics, Railways, Select, Transport, True Crime, Fiction,
Frontline Books, Leo Cooper, Praetorian Press, Seaforth
Publishing, Wharncliffe and White Owl.

For a complete list of Pen & Sword titles please contact

PEN & SWORD BOOKS LIMITED
47 Church Street, Barnsley, South Yorkshire, S70 2AS, England
E-mail: enquiries@pen-and-sword.co.uk
Website: www.pen-and-sword.co.uk

Or
PEN AND SWORD BOOKS
1950 Lawrence Rd, Havertown, PA 19083, USA
E-mail: Uspen-and-sword@casematepublishers.com
Website: www.penandswordbooks.com

CONTENTS

INTRODUCTION

SINCE ITS EARLY days as rolling hills and streams, London has come a long way to be one of the most exciting and innovative cities in the world.

While it's impossible to mention all the incredible buildings that have stood in the capital, this Guide looks at key structures throughout the ages that exemplify the style of the time or have a significance for the city.

From the Romans' first settlement 2,000 years ago, which rose and fell several times before the Roman Empire itself fell, we can still see evidence of their architectural endeavours in amongst the enormously sophisticated buildings of today.

During the Anglo-Saxon period the capital saw more than its fair share of attacks and fighting until the Normans gained power and again started building with purpose. The area boomed under the Tudors and expanded at such pace that the city spilled into the area around the original site of London for the first time.

Houses of Parliament and Big Ben.

By the end of the sixteenth century, more of London's population lived outside the city walls than inside them. The Tudors' timber framed wattle and daub checkerboard houses proliferated.

The Stuart period of the seventeenth century, saw a London that was thriving, with Inigo Jones introducing the classical style of Europe to the city with his magnificent buildings.

The Great Fire struck in 1666, destroying nearly 90 percent of the medieval buildings, but rather than seeing this as a setback, it was used as an opportunity to reimagine the structure of the city. From the ashes rose the magnificent form of St Paul's Cathedral seen today, courtesy of Sir Christopher Wren.

During the Georgian period, London dramatically increased in size again and the style of architecture changed, with the creation of beautiful townhouses, including 10 Downing Street, which would become home for subsequent Prime Ministers.

The Regency period brought new changes, with the prolific architect John Nash designing some of the most famous buildings in London today, including Buckingham Palace and Marble Arch. Victorian Britain was a period of enormous growth, with London becoming a political and financial hub, producing too many innovations and architectural triumphs to mention.

At the advent of the twentieth century there was a change in architectural taste, new materials and grand plans, and Art Deco soon exploded on to the architectural scene.

After the Second World War, London was in desperate need of repair. This devastation was again used as an opportunity to create a better city.

The 1970s brought postmodernism and high tech to architecture in London, and since the Millennium, there has been a wave of spectacular buildings continuing the legacy of original and revolutionary architecture in the capital.

The history of London is a story of experimentation, determination and triumph. A city at the cutting edge of style and fashion, rising from every fire, every attack, every setback. No one can say what the future will hold for the architecture of this fascinating city, but it will almost certainly be surprising, and definitely one to watch.

The London skyline.

CARRERAS CIGARETTE FACTORY

**KING'S CRO
ST PANCR**

ZSL London Zoo

ST JOHN'S
WOOD

Carlton Hill

Abercorn Pl

The Regent's
Park

Robert St

THE BRITISH LIBRARY

Delancey St

Albany St

Outer Cir

Hall Rd

Lord's Cricket Ground

Hampstead Rd

Robert St

Park Rd

Outer Cir

Queen Mary's
Rose Gardens

University of
London

The Sherlock
Holmes Museum

Madame
Tussauds London

SENATE HOUSE BUILDING

BLOOMSBURY

BROADCASTING HOUSE

BEDFORD SQUARE

Westway

A40

PADDINGTON STATION

Seymour Pl

A501

MARYLEBONE

THE BRITISH MUS

The Cartoon Museum

PADDINGTON

George St

A5

John Lewis & Partners

SELFRIDGES

HYDE PARK
ESTATE

Hyde Park Pl

MARBLE ARCH

SOHO

ST GILES

Bayswater Rd

MAYFAIR

ST PAUL'S CHURC

CONV

SIMPSONS OF PICCADILLY

LOND

Princess Diana
Memorial Fountain

Hyde Park

THE RITZ LONDON

THE ATHENAEUM

Kensington Palace

ST JAMES'S PALACE

Pall Mall

ROYAL ALBERT HALL

10 DOWNING STREET

The Mall

HARRODS

Sloane St

BIG BEN

BUCKINGHAM PALACE

Westminster Abbey

NATURAL HISTORY MUSEUM

PALACE OF WESTMINST

BELGRAVIA

WESTMINSTER

Lyall St

Ebury St

Tate Britain

Saatchi Gallery

PIMLICO

ROYAL HOSPITAL CHELSEA

Sutherland St

Millbank

SIS BUILDING

CHELSEA

National Army Museum

Lupus St

CHURCHILL
GARDENS

A3212

CREMORNE
ESTATE

River Thames

BATTERSEA POWER STATION

Nine Elms Ln

LONDINIUM

In ancient times, the area that is now the modern and bustling city of London was mile upon mile of peaceful rolling countryside, crisscrossed with streams. The Romans arrived in AD43 and started building – transforming this tranquil area into Londinium. However, a battle with Boudica saw the new settlement razed to the ground and in its place a more ordered city rose from the ashes. Eventually the London Wall superstructure was built as a defence around the city, and remnants still survive today.

After the invasion nearly 2,000 years ago, Londinium was quickly established as a settlement by the Romans. The city was developed around the area on the River Thames narrow enough to allow the construction of a bridge, but deep enough to handle the seagoing ships of the period, and the remains of an enormous pier base for such a structure were found in 1981 close to the modern London Bridge.

Indeed, evidence suggests the settlement dates back to AD47. A timber drain by the side of the main Roman road excavated at No 1 Poultry has been dated by dendrochronology to this year, thought to be the foundation date of the city.

Following its inception, early Roman London occupied a relatively small area, around 1.4 square kilometres or roughly the area of present-day Hyde Park, and was an area buzzing with activity.

Archaeologists have uncovered numerous goods imported from across the Roman Empire in this period, suggesting that early Roman London was a highly cosmopolitan community of merchants from across the Empire and that local markets existed for such objects.

All was going well for the Roman settlers, but there were problems afoot.

In AD60 or AD61, a little more than ten years after Londinium was founded, the king of the Iceni, a Brittonic tribe set in the east of Britain, died. Until this point the tribe had been largely allowed to live independently, but the death of their king Prasutagus set the country into chaos.

His will had divided his wealth and lands between Rome and his two daughters, but Roman law forbade female inheritance and the king's estate was seized.

Roman financiers called in all the king's outstanding loans at once and the property of both the king and his nobles was taken. The king's wife, Boudica, objected, and the Romans replied by brutally attacking her along with her two daughters. Their nobles and kinsmen were enslaved.

Enraged by the Romans, the popular queen rallied her troops and led a revolt. They destroyed the capital of Camulodunum, which is now known as Colchester, and a mere 15 years after it was created, Londinium was razed to the ground.

However, Boudica and her army were finally defeated by the Romans, and the process to rebuild the city began. In its place a stronger, more ordered city grew.

Towards the end of the first century, Londinium expanded with great speed to become the biggest city in Great Britain, with a population of between 30,000 and 60,000 people. Londinium now replaced Camulodunum as the capital, and even had impressive structures such as a forum and a basilica, which were recorded when the Emperor Hadrian visited in AD122.

Soon after his visit, a major fire ravaged the city and destroyed most of the area. A project began to rebuild, but this time the city would be smaller, housing fewer people.

London Wall

Between the years AD190 and AD225, the ancient city of London was ensconced in one enormous super structure – the London Wall. The structure stretched for two miles from what is now Blackfriars Station in the west to Tower Hill in the east in an arc around the area.

One of the biggest construction projects of Roman Britain, along with Hadrian's Wall, the defence structure survived unchanged, with only a few exceptions, for another 1,700 years.

The Romans were thought to have built the wall as a defence against the Picts, who had recently attacked Hadrian's Wall. Others have suggested it was constructed by the then governor of Britain, Albinus, to protect the area from his rival Septimius Severus.

The structure was between 2.5 and 3 metres wide and up to 6 metres high, and included gateways, towers and ditches. The wall was built from around 85,000 tons of Kentish ragstone, which was brought by barge from quarries near Maidstone.

With more than 20 bastions, mainly around the eastern section, the super structure also had a large 12 acre fort on the north-west area. Home of the

Statue of Roman Emperor Trajan in front of remains of the London Wall.

official guard of the Governor of Britain, the fort would have housed around 1,000 men in a series of barrack blocks. The fort would also have included a series of administrative buildings, stores and other areas, with a ditch or *fossa* in front of the outer wall that stretched up to 5 metres wide and 2 metres deep.

Gateways

The wall's gateways coincided with their alignment to the network of Roman roads that spread across the country. The original gates, clockwise from Ludgate in the west, are Newgate, Cripplegate, Bishopsgate and finally Aldgate in the east. Aldersgate, between Newgate and Cripplegate, was added around AD350, while Moorgate was constructed in the medieval period.

Riverside Wall

The end of the third century brought several attacks on the city from Saxon pirates. In an attempt to prevent this, construction of an additional riverside wall began in AD280 and the wall was repaired around AD390.

This was discovered during excavations at the Tower of London in 1977, which showed that the section of the inner curtain wall between the Lanthorne and Wakefield Towers was originally the eastern part of the Roman riverside wall.

The wall continued to be constructed until at least the end of the fourth century, making it among the last major building projects undertaken by the Romans before their departure from Britain in AD410.

While the area the wall defined has long ago been destroyed or crumbled to dust, there are still remnants of the Roman past visible in London today which can be seen in a few different areas. One of the best places to view the Roman remains is along the boundary of the Square Mile on Tower Hill.

The wall can also be seen further north in the courtyard to the Grange City Hotel on Cooper's Row. More fragments of the wall can be seen along the road named after the Roman structure, London Wall, and the remnants here formed part of a large Roman fort. There are also remains in the gardens of the Barbican.

Remains of the London Wall within the Barbican Estate.

London Wall in the Barbican Estate.

London's Roman amphitheatre

An extraordinary example of Roman architecture can be seen in the basement of the Guildhall Art Gallery. While it had long been thought that Londinium would have had a type of sporting area, London's Roman Amphitheatre was only discovered by archaeologists in 1988, beneath the Guildhall Yard when the gallery was constructed.

Historians were surprised at the location – the majority of ancient amphitheatres were set just outside the city, while this was very much within the old Roman city walls.

The amphitheatre was built in AD70, a simple structure made entirely from wood. During the early part of the second century, the arena was reconstructed to increase its capacity to hold up to 6,000 people.

During this time the arena was used for public events, animal fighting, public executions and, of course, gladiatorial combat.

When the Romans abandoned Britain in the fifth century, the amphitheatre was taken apart and the debris used for building materials. The ruins remained for hundreds of years until the eleventh

London's Roman Amphitheatre (under Guildhall). Wikicommons

century, when the population of London had grown so much that the area simply had to be used again.

To begin with there were basic timber houses, constructed as part of a Viking settlement, before the first ever Guildhall was built on the ancient amphitheatre, making the site a focal point of the city once again.

Today, the amphitheatre lies around 8 metres underground, but above ground there is a line of dark stone that curves in an 80 metre arc to show the edge of the old amphitheatre.

It is possible to see the remains via the Guildhall Art Gallery. Here you can see the fragments of the original walls and the drainage system, as well as the sand used to soak up blood during the gladiatorial battles. A highly impressive digital projection adds to the spectacle by filling in the missing pieces around the remains.

The churches

There are also Roman remains in a couple of churches in the City. All Hallows by the Tower's crypt museum houses a Roman pavement, as well as a wonderful model of Londinium from the 1920s.

Roman Pavement in All Hallows by the Tower Church.

British Museum

In addition to the Museum of London's extensive Roman collection, many artefacts are housed in the British Museum. The Roman Britain display shows hundreds of objects from the era, including many from Londinium, such as mosaics from Leadenhall and the Bank of England, as well as a wooden windlass mechanism and various swords.

2

MEDIEVAL TO THE TUDORS

After the Roman Empire fell, the city changed hands so many times the inhabitants barely knew who was king. With attacks from Vikings and then the Danish, it was a tumultuous time for the country in general and London in particular, but when the Normans finally took over, architecture started to bloom.

The Roman Empire was in rapid decline by the fifth century and the Roman occupation of Britain came to an end in AD410. The city they had built also fell into disrepair, and was abandoned towards the end of the fifth century.

Soon the Anglo-Saxons began to settle in the area of Londinium, with most of the settlement west of the Roman walls in the area that is now the Strand, between Aldwych and Trafalgar Square, and was named Lundenwic. The area was laid out on a grid pattern and was densely occupied with a population thought to be around 10,000 to 12,000.

By the early seventh century the London area was under the control of King Æthelberht of Kent, and it was during this time that the first St Paul's Cathedral was founded. A humble church to begin with, it was destroyed after Æthelberht was driven out of the city by rival King of Essex Saeberht's pagan successors.

During this period London was taken over by various factions, and savagely attacked by the Vikings during the ninth century. For the sake of defence, the settlement moved within the old Roman walls under the rule of King Alfred, and the city became known as Lundenburh, while the old settlement of Lundenwic became known as the Ealdwic or 'old settlement', a name which survives today as Aldwych. The old Roman walls were repaired and the defensive ditch re-cut, while the bridge was probably rebuilt at this time.

From this point, the City of London began to develop its own unique local government. Although it faced competition for political pre-eminence from the traditional West Saxon centre of Winchester, London's size and commercial wealth brought it a steadily increasing importance as a focus of governmental activity.

During the tenth and eleventh centuries, London was attacked by the Danish, and eventually the current King Edmund ceded to King Cnut all of England north of the Thames, including London, and Edmund's death left Cnut in control of the whole country.

Cnut's dynasty ended in 1042 and English rule was restored under Edward the Confessor, who was responsible for the foundation of Westminster Abbey and spent much of his time at Westminster, which from this time steadily supplanted the city itself as the centre of government. Edward's death in 1066 without a clear heir led to a succession dispute and the Norman conquest of England, which resulted in William being crowned king in Westminster Abbey.

During the medieval period, the city was mainly contained by the city walls the Romans had built years earlier, now known as The City of London. Westminster at this time was a separate area to the west of the city, and when the gentry built their elegant houses along the Strand the two communities were connected together.

London Bridge

By the tenth century, there had already been several versions of the famous London Bridge which had been burned down, destroyed or simply crumbled, but it was now reconstructed again, probably from wood. The bridge connected the area with settlements on the south bank of the Thames in Southwark, as

Sketch of the Old Medieval London Bridge.

well as providing links to the south east of England.

The bridge was rebuilt again between 1176 and 1209, and this time it was made from stone. The bridge was around 270 metres long and included 19 arches, a street of shops, as well as houses, a chapel and a drawbridge in the middle, which was included to let large boats pass through, as the River Thames was used as a means of transportation within the city as well as providing access to overseas. There

were a great number of wharfs and quays built along the north bank of the river.

Norman fortresses

The Normans knew great architecture would display their power and control to the Saxon population after their win in the Battle of Hastings in 1066, and so the new regime set to work building defences and establishing their legacy.

They built a number of fortresses along the River Thames towards the centre of London, one of which was Baynard's Castle, which was destroyed in the Great Fire of 1666. The most important of these was the Tower of London at the eastern end of the city, where the initial timber fortification was rapidly replaced by the first stone castle in England.

The Normans brought the new European Romanesque style of architecture to the UK, as well as a great deal more ambition than their predecessors, and their influence marks an important turning point for the capital.

The White Tower

The White Tower is the central keep of the Tower of London series of buildings. Built in a Romanesque style, the tower was completed in the 1080s. Within the building lies the chapel of St John, one of the oldest Romanesque churches in England.

The White Tower.

Chapel of St John the Evangelist inside the White Tower building.

Westminster Hall

Constructed during the reign of William II in 1097, Westminster Hall was intended to be a royal residence, and became the foundation for the Palace of Westminster, which changed and expanded throughout the Middle Ages.

The hall became the largest building of its type in medieval Europe when it was rebuilt under the reign of Richard II, and was considered to be at the forefront of engineering with its pioneering use of an exceptionally wide span hammerbeam roof, added in the fourteenth century.

The hall escaped from the fire of 1834 relatively unscathed, while most of the medieval Palace of Westminster was completely destroyed. Charles Barry and Augustus Pugin redesigned the building and transformed it into the Neo-Gothic Palace of Westminster we have today, while keeping the original Westminster Hall as part of the design.

Westminster Hall is the only surviving medieval part of the Houses of Parliament. istockphoto

Westminster Abbey

While Westminster Abbey was constructed in the reign of Edward the Confessor in the Romanesque tradition, it was rebuilt in the Gothic style in the thirteenth century during the reign of Henry III and this is the version that stands today.

The gothic architecture of the abbey is more similar to French cathedrals, and less like the typical English Gothic of the period.

The Henry VII Chapel was added in the late fifteenth to early sixteenth century, which with its highly ornate fan vaulted ceiling was a spectacular example of late English Gothic architecture.

The building was extended in the eighteenth century when a twin-tower was added to the west of the abbey. Nicholas Hawksmoor designed the Neo-Gothic addition to be of the same style as the rest of the medieval building.

Another significant example of a gothic church that has survived from the Middle Ages is Southwark Cathedral. Originally a former priory, it was the first gothic church in London and built between 1220 and 1420.

Westminster Abbey.

Henry VII Chapel, Westminster Abbey.

Southwark Cathedral.

Tudors

Henry VII, founder of the House of Tudor, became King of England by defeating King Richard III at the Battle of Bosworth Field, the culmination of the War of the Roses.

During the Tudor period, the city expanded rapidly while the economy boomed as there was huge growth in overseas trading. The population grew from around 50,000 in 1500 to 250,000 by 1600. Due to the burgeoning population, the city spilled over into the surrounding areas. By the end of the sixteenth century, more of London's population lived outside the city walls than inside them for the first time.

Hampton Court Palace

The kings of the time, Henry VII then followed by Henry VIII, set upon a variety of extensive royal building projects. This included extending or constructing various palaces, such as Whitehall Palace which stretched from Westminster Hall to what is

Hampton Court Palace.

now Trafalgar Square, as well as the extravagant Nonsuch Palace in Greenwich, and St James's Palace.

However, the most substantial surviving Tudor palace in Greater London is Hampton Court Palace. This was originally built for Cardinal Wolsey and then later became a residence of Henry VIII.

It was greatly extended by Christopher Wren in the late seventeenth century, but the palace retains most of its original Tudor architecture with its sixteenth century great hall, chapel, astronomical clock and gatehouses. It is often regarded as the finest example of Tudor architecture in England.

Aside from constructing beautiful buildings, Henry VIII also influenced the current form of central London by establishing what was originally the hunting grounds of Hyde Park, Green Park and St James's Park, giving London its acres of green spaces.

Beautiful gardens of Hampton Court Palace.

Tudor architecture

This period brought into use the red brick, particularly in large houses and palaces. Examples of this can be seen in the Tudor gatehouse of Lambeth Palace, the London residence of the Archbishop of Canterbury from 1495, Lincoln's Inn from 1521, and St James's Palace from 1536.

Lambeth Palace.

Lincoln's Inn.

St James's Palace.

Staple Inn.

However, one of the most distinctive styles of Tudor architecture were the timber framed wattle and daub houses that had a black and white 'checkerboard' appearance. Most of the commercial and domestic buildings in London before the great fire were built in this style, but only a few remain today.

One such example from the Tudor period is Staple Inn, near Chancery Lane tube station. Another example is 41 Cloth Fair, which was central London's oldest house, and dates back to 1597. Prince Henry's Room, a timber-framed jettied townhouse built in 1610, also survives to this day.

But while many fine examples of Tudor architecture were destroyed in the Great Fire of London, many survived until the nineteenth and twentieth centuries, but were demolished to make way for new development.

THE STUARTS

By the Stuart period of the seventeenth century, London was thriving. Synonymous with architecture of this time is Inigo Jones, who brought the classical style of Europe to the UK in his buildings such as the Banqueting House in Whitehall, Covent Garden and Queen's House in Greenwich.

The Stuart period of British history lasted from 1603 to 1714 during the dynasty of the House of Stuart, which was a period of turmoil and uncertainty caused by in-fighting and religious strife, and a large-scale civil war which resulted in the execution of King Charles I in 1649.

During the early Stuart period a new classical style arrived on the architectural scene in London which had been popularised in Italy in the late fifteenth and early sixteenth centuries.

Inigo Jones

Inigo Jones was a painter, designer, and architect who introduced classical architecture to England.

Born on 15 July 1573 to a cloth worker, Jones was a skilled costume and scenery designer, as well as a gifted architect. He first learned the classical style when travelling around Italy, and was heavily

Inigo Jones.

influenced by Andrea Palladio, an Italian architect who revived the classical style in Italy and explained his theories in *The Four Books on Architecture*. When Jones visited Italy to study the art and architecture, the work of Palladio left an indelible impression.

Jones brought the classical Italian style, characterised by its harmony, detail and proportion, back to England, and was the first to use Vitruvian rules of proportion and symmetry in his buildings. He was appointed Surveyor of the King's Works in 1615, and The Queen's House at Greenwich was his first major work, followed by the Banqueting House at Whitehall, and the Queen's Chapel at St James's Palace.

Jones's full-time career effectively ended with the outbreak of the English Civil War in 1642 and the seizure of the King's houses in 1643. He was captured at the third siege of Basing House in October 1645, and was penalised for his close relationship with Charles I, for which he was heavily fined. He died, penniless, in 1652.

The Banqueting House, Queen's House and St Paul's Covent Garden all survive today. Despite a relatively short career with few works, Jones changed the course of architecture in England by introducing the beauty and elegance of classicism.

Queen's House, Greenwich

Inigo Jones brought a taste of Italian classicism to English architecture with his designs for the beautiful Queen's House in Greenwich.

Jones was commissioned to design the building in 1616 by King James I's wife, Anne of Denmark. Legend has it that this was intended as a gift from the king – a rather flamboyant apology for swearing in front of her after she had

Queen's House, Greenwich.

accidentally killed one of his favourite dogs during a hunt.

However, Anne of Denmark died three years later in 1619, by which time only the first floor had been completed, and she did not see Jones's revolutionary design realised.

Work halted on the grand building, only restarting in 1629, when James's son Charles I gave the Queen's House to his wife Henrietta Maria. The magnificent building was finally finished in 1636 and became the first fully Classical building in England.

It is noted for its symmetrical shape, elegant proportions and interiors, and revolutionary in its break from the typical Tudor red-brick style of architecture that was popular at the time. The style of the new building was so unusual, it was known simply as 'The White House'.

The Great Hall and Tulip Stairs
At the heart of the Queen's House is the Great Hall, which is a perfect cube in shape and has a first-floor gallery overlooking a black-and-white marble floor. The ceiling of the Great Hall was originally adorned with paintings by Orazio and Gentileschi. However, these artworks were later moved to Marlborough House.

Famous features include the Tulip Stairs – an intricate wrought iron spiral

Tulip Staircase at Queen's House.

stairway that weaves up through the building, below a glass dome. This was the very first spiral stair in Britain that was not centrally supported – each tread is cantilevered from the wall and then supported by the stair below.

The spectacular building also included a balcony from which the Queen and her ladies would watch the riding and hunting that took place in the park.

Although the house was a triumph that would redefine architecture in England, Henrietta Maria would not have a great deal of time to enjoy her new building. The Civil War started in 1642 and she was forced to flee. Her husband, Charles I, was executed and soon after, his property was seized by the state. After the restoration, Henrietta Maria would eventually return in 1660.

From the 1670s onwards the Queen's House was mainly used as a residence for royal servants and artists, including the van de Veldes, who came to London from Holland by Royal invitation in 1672.

In the eighteenth century, many renowned architects took inspiration from Jones's designs and classical architectural in general, such as Lord Burlington, Colen Campbell and William Kent, and fused into the Georgian style, now seen all across the country.

The Queen's House was still used by members of the royal family until 1805, when King George III allowed the building to be used as a school by a charity for the orphans of seamen, called the Royal Naval Asylum. This remained until 1933, when the school moved to Suffolk, and the building was taken over by the National Maritime Museum in 1934.

The Queen's House is still known today for its impressive art collection which includes works by Great Masters such as Gainsborough, Reynolds, Turner and Hogarth.

Banqueting House in Whitehall

Jones's next major work in London was the Banqueting House in Whitehall, built between 1619 and 1622. There had been two Banqueting Houses

Banqueting House in Whitehall.

before this, one for Elizabeth I, constructed mainly from timber, bricks and canvas, which had been very popular with Elizabeth's successor, James, and his wife Anne of Denmark, as a place to host masques, a type of courtly entertainment.

The King eventually commissioned a more substantial building to replace the current one, but was disappointed with the result. Although beautiful and ornate, a series of columns blocked a large section of the audience's view.

James had appointed Inigo Jones as his new Surveyor of the King's Works, and chose him to replace the Banqueting House with a grand building, one that would do the masques justice.

Inigo Jones drew up plans for a completely different type of classical building, using inspiration from his travels to inject the classicism of ancient Rome and the Renaissance into his design. The impressive Banqueting House building was completed in 1622 – and the King was delighted with the result.

The new structure was an extension to the Palace of Whitehall, and featured a Palladian Portland stone facade, as well as a spectacular ceiling decorated with nine paintings by the famous Flemish painter Rubens, which remain on the ceiling today. Jones's Banqueting House was a perfectly proportioned masterpiece – a revolution in architecture.

Covent Garden

The next project was possibly Jones's most important work yet – the redevelopment of Covent Garden.

The Earl of Bedford was given permission to redevelop an area of land he owned north of the Strand. He aspired to create elegant new housing that would attract wealthy tenants to Covent Garden, and commissioned Jones in 1630 to completely redesign this area. Jones designed London's first modern square and the resulting area was a classical style piazza lined with grand terraced houses.

The Earl felt he had to include a church in the design, but instructed Jones he just wanted to add a simple church that was 'not much better than a barn'. Jones famously replied, 'Then you shall have the finest barn in Europe.'

It was a very special barn indeed – Jones's design for the church used Vitruvius's template for a Tuscan temple. St Paul's Church would be the first church in England to be built entirely in the classical style. The church is the centrepiece of the piazza, and sits on the west side of the square, featuring a grand Tuscan-style portico.

The church was completed in 1633 at a cost of £4,886, but the church hierarchy were not happy with the design. Jones had planned for the main entrance to be through the spectacular portico from the piazza. However, the church insisted that the doorways

St Paul Church, Covent Garden.

Jones had designed should be blocked and the entrance was moved to the more simple west side through the church yard.

The church has a long association with the theatre community and is known as the actors' church. Indeed, on 9 May 1662, Samuel Pepys made a diary entry about the first 'Italian puppet play' that was set under the church portico. The magnificent portico was also the setting for the first scene of Shaw's *Pygmalion*. Many well known musicians, artists and actors have memorials in the church, including Charlie Chaplin, Noël Coward, Vivien Leigh and Ivor Novello.

Jones's design for the area was extremely popular and copies of the fashionable piazza soon appeared across the city, with a great number of trendy squares built in the West End of London during the Georgian period.

The style of the Church of St Paul was also very popular and Christopher Wren used this as inspiration for other city churches created after the Great Fire of London.

Covent Garden market.

4

THE GREAT FIRE

Disaster struck in 1666 as fire ravaged the city, destroying nearly 90 percent of the medieval buildings. However, this offered the opportunity to revolutionise the structure of the city, and architects such as Sir Christopher Wren rose to the challenge with buildings such as St Paul's Cathedral and Royal Chelsea Hospital.

On 2 September 1666, Thomas Farriner, a baker on Pudding Lane was about to dramatically change the course of history. Soon after midnight, a fire started in his bakery and spread west, swiftly whipping through the City of London and creating chaos and damage on a scale never seen before in the area.

The wind fanned the bakery fire into a firestorm that pushed north the next day into the heart of the City and continued until 6 September. The fire spread across the central parts of the area, destroying St Paul's Cathedral, and the medieval City of London inside the old Roman wall, and even expanded across the River Fleet, nearly reaching King Charles II's Palace of Whitehall.

The fire devastated the city and the battle to put the fire out was long and arduous. Eventually the fire died down thanks to the strong easterly winds abating and the efforts of the Tower of London garrison, who used gunpowder to create effective firebreaks to halt further spread towards the east.

But the damage had been done. The death toll was unknown but thought to have been relatively low and only six verified deaths were recorded. But the impact on the city was enormous – the Great Fire destroyed approximately ninety per cent of the medieval city, which included around 87 parish churches, 44 Company Halls, the Royal Exchange, the Custom House, Old St Paul's Cathedral, the Bridewell Palace and other City prisons, the General Letter Office, and the three western city gates: Ludgate, Newgate, and

Vintage woodcut of the Great Fire.

Aldersgate, as well as the majority of the homes of the city's inhabitants.

Archaeologists later found a melted piece of pottery in Pudding Lane where the fire started, now on display at the Museum of London. The melted pottery showed that the temperature of the fire had reached 1,250°C.

The fire created social and economic problems on a scale never seen before. King Charles II encouraged the new refugees to flee from London to find refuge in settlements elsewhere as he feared riots would ensue if the now homeless Londoners stayed.

Monument to the Great Fire of London.

While the Great Fire caused so much destruction, it also created a unique opportunity to redesign the formerly primitive and mainly medieval city.

Rebuilding the city

Architects such as Christopher Wren put together radical plans to reconstruct the city in a classical style. These plans suggested completely redesigning the city and doing away with the rather chaotic street plan of the medieval period, and replacing it with a grid system replete with piazzas, wide boulevards and a classical style for any new buildings.

However, these grand plans were not to be for many reasons including a lack of labour force, as well as the urgent need to rebuild the city as soon as feasible, and so the city was constructed around the original medieval street plans.

Although the new plans for the city were watered down considerably, the reconstruction saw the city undergo a radical transformation with a fresh style not seen before in London – architectural uniformity. Charles II specified in 1667 that all new houses were to be built to a specific height and plot size, and should be built from brick rather than wood to reduce the risk of another great fire.

Due to this decree, the ramshackle streets from the Stuart era with overhanging timber framed houses were replaced with uniform rows of carefully proportioned brick terraces, such as the simple houses at King's Bench Walk in the Inner Temple, which were built immediately after the fire and became a blueprint for the typical Georgian terraced house.

King's Bench Walk.

St Paul's Cathedral

The pearl in the crown, however, was Wren's reconstruction of St Paul's Cathedral, the fifth such building on the site of Ludgate Hill. The original church was founded in AD604, and rebuilt several times until the fourth version, also known as Old St. Paul, which was an enormous Gothic cathedral with a tower and a spire constructed by the Normans and widely thought to be one of the masterpieces of medieval Europe, was severely damaged by the Great Fire.

It was decided to build an entirely new cathedral from scratch and Wren was given the task of creating a fitting replacement for the Old St. Paul's. Taking inspiration from contemporary Renaissance trends in Italian architecture, Wren designed the cathedral with muted elements of the Baroque style. He combined the tradition of English cathedrals with the classicism of Inigo Jones's masterpieces as well as French buildings by Mansart. The dome of the cathedral also echoes the features of St Peter's Basilica in Rome.

St Paul's Cathedral.

With the original plan, Wren wanted to construct the cathedral on a Greek cross layout, but this was rejected, and he was forced to change the design to the Latin cross layout of the former gothic cathedral instead. He designed the impressive west facade to be fronted by a wide welcoming flight of steps, a two-storey portico and two Baroque towers.

The famous lead-covered dome is one of the world's largest, and with the cathedral reaching a height of 111 metres, it was the tallest building in London from its completion in 1710 until 1963.

One of the unusual features of St. Paul's is its crypt which continues under the entire building, as opposed to just the eastern end which is more common in cathedrals. The crypt holds the secret to the construction of the magnificent building, as it actually has a structural purpose, with huge piers that spread the weight of the cathedral's slimmer piers, necessary due to London's weak clay soil.

The construction of the cathedral took over 40 years, with the 'topping out' taking place in 1708. Wren's son, Christopher Wren Jr, placed the final stone on the lantern, watched by his father from below.

The results speak for themselves – the cathedral is generally thought to be one of the greatest ever constructed, and this landmark became a symbol of London, synonymous with the capital itself.

The spectacular building has been the location for the funerals of Lord Nelson, the Duke of Wellington and Sir Winston Churchill, as well as the wedding of Prince Charles and Lady Diana.

The city churches

Wren was also charged with the design of a total of 51 churches in the city and 25 of these still stand today. Eclectic and creative, these churches were frequently built on very small, restricted sites and feature striking towers.

One of the most interesting examples is the tiered spire of St Bride's Fleet Street, one of the tallest of the city churches. The tower of St-Mary-le-bow is another famous example combining gothic elements with classicism.

Wren was known for combining different styles to great effect, which St Peter Upon Cornhill illustrates with a mix of Dutch classicism and Palladianism. St Mary Aldermary on the other hand, is a purely neo-gothic recreation of the former medieval church that stood on that same spot in the late Middle Ages.

Wren's biggest achievement however, was the prolific nature of his work. He helped to transform the skyline of London with the tall spires and domes of his churches soaring far above the rest of the city.

St Bride's Church.

St Mary Aldermary.

The Great Fire was a tragedy, yet from the embers grew a vastly improved and modernised city. It was a fresh start, giving the planners a chance to devise a masterplan, with new types of housing and elegant streets dotted with impressive buildings and opulent churches. The reconstruction of London made it more modern, uniform and cleaner than all the other cities in Europe during that period.

Public buildings

Wren was also responsible for the design of two new military hospitals – the Royal Hospital Chelsea and the Old Royal Naval College, now known as Greenwich Hospital.

The Royal Chelsea Hospital, completed in 1692, is a fine example of Wren's more simple style, featuring a red brick facade, as well as a

Royal Hospital Chelsea.

Old Royal Naval College.

Christ Church in Spitalfields.

handsome chapel and great hall. On the opposite end of the spectrum, the highly ornate Old Royal Naval College, completed in 1712, shows Wren's more opulent styling with its exquisite Painted Hall and St Paul's Chapel, as well as the symmetrical east and west wings which frame Queens House, designed by Inigo Jones. Now a designated UNESCO World Heritage Site, the buildings are thought to be the pinnacle of the English Baroque movement.

Nicholas Hawksmoor

In 1710, an act of Parliament requested 50 new churches to be constructed in London. This was an ambitious demand, and only 12 of these, known as the Commissioner's Churches, were actually built, the majority of which were designed by the former assistant of Christopher Wren, Nicholas Hawksmoor.

Hawksmoor had previously worked on the city churches and Old Royal Naval College, and was well known for his rather idiosyncratic style which drew influence from architecture across the globe and from all periods – Roman, Greek, Egyptian and medieval designs. One of the most famous churches he designed is Christ Church in Spitalfields, completed in 1729, a fine example of Hawksmoor's trademark fusion of gothic and baroque elements.

Christopher Wren

Christopher Wren, born 20 October 1632, was by turns a designer, astronomer, geometrician, anatomist, and, of course, one of the greatest English architects of all time. In total, Wren designed a total of 52 London churches, including St Paul's Cathedral, as well as many other significant buildings. He studied Latin and Aristotelian physics at the University of Oxford, and was a founder of the Royal Society – his scientific work was admired by Isaac Newton and Blaise Pascal. He was knighted for his efforts in 1673.

Christopher Wren.

THE GEORGIANS

From 1714 to 1837, London dramatically increased in size and the style of architecture changed with the creation of beautiful townhouses. The Scottish architect Colen Campbell set the tone for this new type of building and became known as the 'father of the Georgian style'.

During the Georgian period, Britain experienced enormous changes in the form of economic and colonial expansion. The country emerged from this as an important trading power in the global arena, and London lay at the centre of its power and influence. This new found wealth had an enormous impact on the city, which grew quickly and sprawled across new areas as the population exploded in the eighteenth century.

There was a great deal of new construction in areas such as Kensington, Mayfair, Marylebone and Bloomsbury to the west of the city. Development also flourished in villages around London, including Hackney, Dulwich, Hampstead and Islington.

In these areas, style was key. Fashionable terraces and trendy squares were built such as Bedford Square, Grosvenor Square and Portman Square, and the new middle classes that emerged from Britain's economic growth flocked to these areas.

Along with these highly covetable squares, new bridges were built connecting the north and south banks of the Thames, at Westminster in 1750 and Blackfriars in 1769. These were the first new bridges to be constructed since the early Middle Ages, and with this new development the city began to spread south of the river.

Colen Campbell

Scottish architect Colen Campbell was very influential during this period. His book *Vitruvius Britannicus* set the tone and style for English architecture during the eighteenth century, and he became known as the 'father of the Georgian style'.

The Georgian style prized simple brickwork and put an emphasis on geometry. Typical Georgian terraced houses have a few common traits. They usually include sunken basements, and reception rooms with taller ceilings. They are generally built from pale yellow London stock brick, which often appears grey, and have tall panelled front doors flanked by columns.

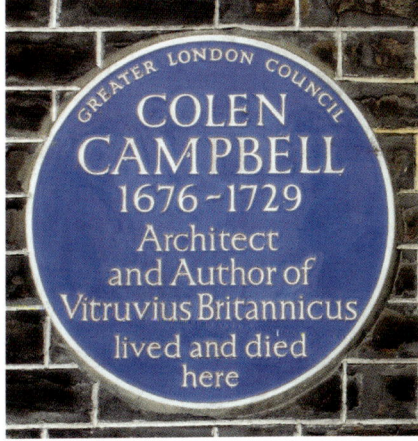

Colen Campbell. Wikicommons

They also featured triple bay frontages and carefully proportioned, very large off-white sash windows. The sashes allowed the window to be held open on corded lead weights to ventilate the room. This new feature was originally developed in Holland and was first seen in the Royal palaces, but became very popular in Georgian times and replaced casement windows as the norm. The frames of these windows were designed to be as slim as possible, allowing the biggest sheets of glass available for the space so light could flood into the rooms.

These handsome houses were situated in the new sought-after squares, crescents and terraces such as Bedford Square, Grosvenor Square and Portman Square, which often had wide pavements and private access to beautifully landscaped gardens.

Bedford Square.

Each house was designed with the modern family in mind – the ground floor was for business, the principal floor was for formal entertaining, and upper storeys held family bedrooms. Servants lived in the attic rooms and worked in the basement kitchen, hurrying between floors as required. Every level had a different height to indicate its intended use and also its relative importance.

Chimney breasts were located in shared party walls, and the more chimney pots visible on the roof indicated the wealth of the inhabitants – many chimney pots meant there were fireplaces in every room.

However, outwardly the houses were simple and avoided the adornments seen in continental architecture of the time.

10 Downing Street

The official residence of the UK prime minister and the headquarters of the British Government is 10 Downing Street, set in the London borough of the City of Westminster.

Commonly referred to as Number 10, it is a classic example of simple Georgian architecture, constructed from London stock brick and featuring the trademark Georgian sash windows, as well as the Georgian front door

Entrance of 10 Downing Street.

with fanned light above, surrounded by columns.

The building houses around 100 rooms, with the private residence on the third floor, and the kitchen in the basement. The other floors are made up of offices, conference rooms, lounges and dining rooms. There is an interior courtyard, as well as a terrace and a garden of 2,000 square metres.

History of Downing Street

In 1654, Sir George Downing acquired the lease on the land just to the south of St James's Park, and adjacent to a mansion that overlooked the area. His aim? To construct a row of attractive townhouses 'for persons of good quality to inhabit in'. It seemed a simple idea, but a dispute over the land delayed the project by nearly 30 years

The townhouses were designed by the eminent and prolific architect Sir Christopher Wren, and construction began in 1682. Over the next two years, a cul-de-sac of two-storey Georgian townhouses complete with stables and coach houses were built. The houses were constructed in haste on soil that was soft and with shallow foundations that would prove to be problematic in time – Winston Churchill would later say that Number 10 was 'shaky and lightly built by the profiteering contractor whose name they bear'.

A variety of distinguished and wealthy people moved into the new cul-de-sac, but Downing himself never

Downing Street.

lived in Downing Street. He moved to Cambridge in 1675 and died in 1684, just a few months after construction on Downing Street had finished. Downing's portrait hangs in the entrance hall of Number 10.

Johann Caspar von Bothmer, adviser to George I and George II, took up residency at Number 10 in 1720, and although he complained about the condition of the house, he lived there until his death in 1732. Bothmer was the first politician to reside in 10 Downing Street and when he died, ownership reverted to the Crown.

In 1732, William Kent, an eminent English architect, painter and furniture designer set about reforming the interior, and it was at this time that the building's most iconic architectural feature, the stone staircase, was added. The beautiful staircase weaves its way from the ground level to the third floor, with a wrought iron balustrade featuring a scroll design, as well as a mahogany handrail.

It was in 1735 that King George II gave the house to Robert Walpole, regarded as the very first prime minister of the country, as a gift for his services to the nation. The king had also obtained the leases on two other Downing Street properties and added these to his proposed gift.

Walpole, however, was uncomfortable accepting the property as a gift and suggested the houses should become the official residence of the office of the First Lord of the Treasury. Walpole would live there as the incumbent First Lord, but would vacate the property for the next one.

He used the ground floor for business, while the largest room on the north-west side of the house became his study, and is now the Cabinet Room. While Walpole lived at Number 10 for another seven years until 1742, when he left the office of prime minister his replacement, Spencer Compton, was not keen to take over the residency of the house. Indeed, it was 21 years before another prime minister would live at Number 10.

It was rather unpopular with subsequent prime ministers as it was rather small compared to other townhouses in central London. It was also in fairly poor condition, and due to the flaws in the foundations, the house had begun to sink over the years, causing all kinds of problems such as cracked walls and chimneys, as well as buckled floors.

Walpole's successors such as Prime Minister Henry Pelham preferred to live in their own residences. In 1763 George Grenville took up residence briefly before he was sacked by King George III in 1765. The next prime minister to move into Downing Street was Lord North, who was extremely fond of the house and implemented a great many improvements during his time at Number 10.

In the 1770s, the six-panelled Georgian-style front door was fitted. It was made from black oak and designed by the architect Kenton Couse. He also had the black and white chequerboard floor in the entrance hall installed, as well as the lamp above the front door and the famous lion's head door knocker.

After North resigned, his successors continued to use Number 10 as the prime minister's office, but most chose to live in their own townhouses.

No one had lived in 10 Downing Street for 30 years when the new Prime Minister Benjamin Disraeli arrived in 1868, and he described it as being 'dingy and decaying'. Over the following few decades, the building was renovated and transformed. Electric lighting and the first telephones were installed during William Gladstone's premiership in 1884, while central heating was fitted in 1937 and the attic

rooms were converted into a prime ministerial flat.

When Arthur Balfour became Prime Minister in 1902, Number 10 was in good shape and he decided to use the refurbished building as his official residence, and this has remained the custom ever since.

More problems were to come, however, and by the 1950s the building was in serious need of renovation as there were significant structural issues, such as the staircase shrinking, pervasive dry rot throughout and a risk of the load bearing walls collapsing.

Then prime minister Harold Macmillan instructed a committee to investigate in 1958, resulting in an extensive overhaul. This took three years to complete and cost £1 million, which was a whole year past the deadline and £500,000 over budget.

Downing Street in the winter.

During Margaret Thatcher's tenure in the 1980s, further extensive repairs were commissioned, and again during the time of Tony Blair and David Cameron. Since Blair held the office, however, prime ministers have chosen to live in the larger flat at number 11 Downing Street, which was traditionally the residence of the chancellor.

Somerset House

One of the most spectacular pieces of Georgian architecture can be found in Somerset House, a Neoclassical building set on the Strand, overlooking the River Thames. The magnificent Georgian building was constructed on the site of a former Tudor palace, built for the Duke of Somerset in the sixteenth century.

William Chambers designed the new building to be arranged in a quadrangle with a courtyard in the centre, and the project was completed in 1776. The building was extended in Victorian times to add wings to the east and west sections.

While the Georgian building was intended as a grand public building to house a variety of government and public service offices, it presently houses various organisations centred around the arts and education.

Somerset House.

REGENCY STYLES

A brief but architecturally important time was the Regency period, where new styles were developed. Architect John Nash was prolific at this time, designing some of the most famous buildings in London today, including Buckingham Palace and Marble Arch.

Although the Regency period covers just the nine years between 1811 and 1820, when the Prince Regent, later to become George IV, ruled as proxy for his ill father, George III, the architectural trends established during this time continued well into the nineteenth century.

The eldest child of King George III and Queen Charlotte, George IV led an extravagant lifestyle which influenced the fashions of that era enormously. He commissioned several significant buildings such as the Royal Pavilion in Brighton by John Nash, as well as the remodelling of Buckingham Palace, and he also arranged for Windsor Castle to be rebuilt.

Regency architecture fuses the ornaments of Graeco-Roman architecture, such as friezes, statues, urns and porticos, with the symmetry and clean lines of the Georgian style. Georgian features such as sash windows were also incorporated, and first floor balconies became very popular during this period as well.

One of the biggest differences between Georgian and Regency architecture lies in the facade of buildings. While exposed brick was fashionable in early Georgian times, the Regency style favoured covering exposed brick with stucco painted in cream tones, in imitation of natural stone or marble.

Decimus Burton

Decimus Burton, an architect who specialised in Greek Revival, was responsible for designing luxury developments of terraces in Regent's Park, such as Cornwall, Clarence and York. But it was his design for the Athenaeum Club, built in 1830 with a frieze based on the recently acquired Elgin Marbles in the British Museum, that really caught people's attention.

Decimus Burton. Wikicommons

The Athenaeum was a club founded in 1824 for 'Literary and Scientific men and followers of the Fine Arts'. The club first rented a building temporarily before deciding to commission the 24-year-old Decimus Burton to design a permanent clubhouse.

Constructed in the Neoclassical style, with a wild mix of influences from Ancient Greece, Rome, and Egypt, along with Renaissance Italian elements, Burton's spectacular building for the Athenaeum club has a Doric portico with paired columns, as well as a beautiful central staircase. Burton took control of as many features of the building as possible, inside and out, even down to the clock-cases and the pendant light-fittings.

Athenaeum Club.

The Athenaeum club committee were ecstatic with the results, and Burton became the 'prime member' of the Athenaeum, one of London's grandest gentlemen's clubs.

Buckingham Palace

The official London residence of the UK's sovereigns since 1837 and today the administrative headquarters of the Monarch, Buckingham Palace is one of the most prestigious addresses in the world.

The first house on the site was built around 1624, but the building that sits at the centre of the modern palace was known as Buckingham House, a large townhouse built for the Duke of Buckingham in 1703, replacing the original house. Designed by William Winde, it featured a large, three-storey central block with two smaller flanking service wings.

In 1761, King George III acquired the house as a private residence for Queen Charlotte and began to remodel the structure, but it was in 1826 that King George IV decided to transform the house into a palace, using the services of the architect John Nash.

One of the eminent architects of the Regency period, John Nash designed some of the most spectacular buildings in London today. As well as many handsome residential terraces, Nash was responsible for transforming the modest Buckingham House from George III's reign into Buckingham Palace, a grand Neoclassical palace, under the flamboyant Prince Regent's instruction.

Buckingham Palace.

Aerial view of Buckingham Palace.

Parliament gave the king a budget of £150,000, but he insisted on £450,000 to complete the works. Nash began the work in 1825, extending the existing house by adding three wings around a central courtyard. The Palace was constructed in Bath stone, which has a golden tone, rather than the stucco-faced brick Nash used on previous work.

With a two-storey porch combining Doric columns and tall Corinthian columns above, statues, and sculpture, the front facade of the main building is a triumph of Regency Neoclassicism. There is also a frieze with decorative scrollwork, and sculptures inspired by the Elgin Marbles.

The design was luxurious in the extreme and the costs ballooned. The King removed Nash from the project three years later in 1829. When the new monarch, King William IV, took over in 1830, he appointed Edward Blore to finish the building work.

The king never moved into the Palace, and he even offered the building to Parliament when the Houses of Parliament were destroyed by fire in 1834, but the offer was declined.

It was when Queen Victoria took the throne in 1837 that Buckingham Palace became the official London residence of the British monarch. The palace was extended and renovated

The Victoria Memorial statue.

again after her marriage to add more space for nurseries and bedrooms for guests.

In 1883, the ultimate luxury – electricity – was installed, first transforming the Ball Room. In 1911, the gates, railings and forecourt were added, while in 1913, Sir Aston Webb redesigned the east front that overlooks the Mall, adding a facade of Portland stone to provide a backdrop to the Victoria Memorial statue, as well as the balcony – one of the most famous in the world.

Balcony of Buckingham Palace.

The first known Royal balcony appearance took place in 1851, when Queen Victoria stepped out during celebrations for the opening of the Great Exhibition. The Royal family have appeared on the balcony several times since then, during occasions such as the Queen's annual official birthday celebrations to watch the RAF flypast at the end of Trooping the Colour, as well as Royal Weddings, and many national celebrations such as the 75th anniversary of the Battle of Britain.

The palace now has more than 77,000 square metres of floor space, with 775 rooms, which include 19 state rooms, 52 principal bedrooms, 188 staff bedrooms, 92 offices, and 78 bathrooms. It also has its own post office, cinema, swimming pool, doctor's surgery and jeweller's workshop, as well as the largest private garden in London. The interior includes a mix of baroque and rococo, along with nineteenth century finishes.

During the Second World War, the palace was bombed nine times, and John Mowlem & Co. was employed to carefully restore the palace to its former glory when the war was over. In 1970, the palace was designated a Grade I listed building.

Over the years, the palace began to fall into disrepair until in 2017 Parliament approved a schedule of works to transform the buildings. The work included new plumbing, wiring, boilers, radiators and solar panel installation on the roof at an estimated cost of £369 million, funded by the income from the Crown Estate.

Buckingham Palace is very much a working building today and the centre of the monarchy. It is the venue for royal events and ceremonies – from lavish receptions to entertaining foreign heads of state. Around 50,000 people visit the Palace each year as guests to State banquets, lunches, dinners, receptions and garden parties. It is also at the Palace that the Queen holds weekly audiences with the prime minister.

The Palace is also a family home. This is where the Queen gave birth to Prince Charles and Prince Andrew, the place where The Prince of Wales, The Princess Royal, The Duke of York and Prince William were christened, and also the site of many celebrations of Royal Weddings, most recently that of the Duke and Duchess of Cambridge.

Marble Arch

Commissioned by King George IV, Marble Arch was designed by architect John Nash to be a grand gateway to the ever expanding Buckingham Palace and a celebration of British victories in the Napoleonic Wars.

However, after the death of George IV placed William IV on the throne, the project was reassessed. William IV

Marble Arch.

believed the cost of the arch was simply too great, and consequently the work was completed in 1833 with parts of the initial design missing, including a statue of George IV.

When the palace was expanded under Queen Victoria's reign, Marble Arch was carefully dismantled and rebuilt on the corner of Hyde Park, where it became an entrance to the area. However, as London continued to grow, it was felt that the roads needed to be widened and Marble Arch is now separated from Hyde Park.

Marble Arch is still used in royal processions, and the gold state coach passed through the gate during Queen Elizabeth II's coronation in 1953.

British Museum

Set in the Bloomsbury area of London, the British Museum is one of the largest in the world, housing an estimated eight million works and attracting over five million visitors each year.

From humble beginnings, the museum was based entirely on the collections of the scientist Sir Hans Sloane, and opened to the public in 1759. As the collection expanded, the museum grew to house the precious artefacts.

The British Museum.

In 1823, the eminent architect Sir Robert Smirke designed the core of the building in the Greek Revival style, planned as a quadrangle featuring four wings. This style had become more popular as the British began to explore sites in Ancient Greece in the late eighteenth century.

There were many decorative features incorporated in the design. Smirke drew inspiration from the temple of Athena Polias at Priene and added 44 columns in the Ionic order, each 14 metres high. He also designed the pediment along the south entrance which comprises sculptures illustrating the 'progress of civilisation', with a series of 15 allegorical figures. The quadrangle won the RIBA Gold Medal soon after its completion in 1852.

Sydney Smirke

The brother of Robert Smirke, Sydney designed Weston Hall in 1845, again using inspiration from the patterns and colour palette of classical Greek buildings for the ceiling. He was also responsible for the design of the Reading Room at the centre of the Great Court, which features a dome inspired by the Pantheon with a diameter of around 42.6 metres.

Decorative facade of the British Museum.

The dome was built in sections on a cast iron framework, while the ceiling was constructed from papier mâché and suspended on struts hanging from the frame.

The book shelves that surround the spectacular room were 3 miles long, and constructed from iron to hold the considerable weight of the books, and also to reduce the risk of fire.

The interior was painstakingly restored during the late-twentieth century redevelopment of the Great Court, where the original blue, cream and gold colour scheme and the papier mâché was restored.

Great Court

The Reading Room was originally at the centre of the museum, surrounded by a courtyard garden, but this changed in 1997 when the entire library section was moved to the British Library, leaving an enormous gap in the British Museum.

A competition was staged to redesign the courtyard, long thought to be congested and overly complicated. The winner emerged as architect Norman Foster, who then proceeded to completely transform the space into the largest covered public square in Europe with an incredible roof made from steel and glass.

The design was based loosely around Norman Foster's idea for the roof of the Reichstag in Berlin. Work began in 1999, and 3,212 panes of glass were constructed, all entirely unique and of varying shapes. It was completed in 2000 and the new design gave visitors the chance to move around the main area of the museum freely for the first time in over 150 years.

The Reading Room, British Museum.

The Great Court of the British Museum.

THE VICTORIANS

Victorian Britain was a period of enormous growth, with London becoming a political and financial centre, which was reflected in the architecture. At this point a whole host of spectacular buildings were created, such as the Houses of Parliament, Big Ben, the Royal Albert Hall, Leadenhall Market, the Natural History Museum and more.

The Victorian era, from 1837 to 1901, marked a highly prolific time in terms of architecture. As the British Empire grew, London rose to become the first metropolis and there was simply unprecedented growth in the increasingly urbanised capital. London was now the political and financial centre of the world's biggest Empire. The architecture had to live up to this new found position of power and affluence.

Palace of Westminster

The Palace of Westminster, otherwise known as the Houses of Parliament, is one of the most iconic buildings in the world. Set along the River Thames, the Houses of Parliament consists of the House of Commons and the House of Lords. The current incarnation of the building was designed in the Gothic tradition by architect Charles Barry along with Augustus Pugin, and constructed between 1840 and 1870.

The site on the north bank of the Thames was originally known as Thorney Island, and a hotbed of royal power from as far back as the Middle Ages. The newly crowned Edward the Confessor ordered the first palace to be built on the site in the tenth century. This was closely followed by the nearby Westminster Abbey. Under the reign of William II, the original Great Hall was built, completed in 1099.

In Anglo-Saxon times, the capital was Winchester, but this began to change, and the Parliament met for the first time in Westminster at the palace in 1295.

The Palace acted as the monarch's place of residence during the late medieval period, and new buildings and courts were built, but a fire ravaged the area in 1512, destroying

Palace of Westminster.

the residential area of the palace, and King Henry VIII was forced to move elsewhere.

Gunpowder Plot

On 5 November 1605, the palace was the target of an assassination attempt as a group of English Catholics tried to blow up the House of Lords. An anonymous tip off alerted the police and Guy Fawkes was found hiding in the Lords with several barrels of gunpowder. This near miss is now celebrated with an annual Bonfire Night on 5 November.

As the Parliament grew and developed, the Palace became less and less suitable for purpose. Construction work began to enlarge the buildings between 1824 and 1827, when new library facilities and law courts were added.

Another fire spread through the palace in October 1834, and while Westminster Hall escaped unscathed, the Lords and Commons Chambers needed to be completely rebuilt.

Many different designs were suggested for the replacement buildings, but the Royal Commission chose Charles Barry's Perpendicular Gothic plan, as the Gothic revival design embodied the traditional conservative values of the time. Augustus Pugin, an expert on the Gothic style, joined the team to help with detailing and features such as the spires and vanes. The new Lords Chamber was completed by 1847, the Commons Chamber soon after in 1852, with the full construction completed in 1870.

The result is a masterclass in Gothic architecture with beautiful elements such as 'tracery', a form of delicate, web-like ornamentation for windows and parapets. Other gothic features used include a strong symmetry of lines, pointed arches, spires and steep roofs.

The palace now houses over 1,100 rooms, 100 staircases and 3 miles of passageways. The main features include the grand entrance of the Norman Porch, the Queen's Robing Room where the sovereign prepares for the state opening of Parliament, and the Royal Gallery. Westminster Hall is the oldest existing part of the Palace, and now used mainly for ceremonial purposes.

The Palace is one of the busiest Parliaments in the world, and has more than a million visitors each year.

Big Ben

The most iconic feature of the Houses of Parliament is the Elizabeth Tower, more commonly known by the name of its bell, Big Ben. The official name of the tower was originally the Clock Tower, but it was renamed Elizabeth Tower in 2012 to mark the Diamond Jubilee of Queen Elizabeth II.

This was also designed by Augustus Pugin in a Neo-Gothic style, and when the magnificent tower was completed in 1859, its clock was the largest and

Big Ben.

most accurate four-faced striking and chiming clock in the world. The structure stands 96 metres tall, and has 334 steps from the ground floor to the belfry.

Dials of the clock are 7 metres in diameter, and Big Ben, the largest of the tower's five bells, weighs 13.7 tonnes – it was the largest bell in the UK for 23 years. Four quarter bells chime at 15, 30 and 45 minutes past the hour and just before Big Ben tolls on the hour. The clock uses its original Victorian mechanism, but an electric motor can be used as a backup.

The bell's nickname is thought to come from one of two origins – it is either named after Sir Benjamin Hall, who oversaw its installation, or the heavyweight boxing champion Benjamin Caunt.

The iconic clock tower has been Grade I listed since 1970 and a UNESCO World Heritage Site since 1987.

The Royal Albert Hall

Set to the south of Hyde Park in South Kensington, the Royal Albert Hall is one of the UK's most famous performance venues, holding the Proms classical concerts every year since 1941. Queen Victoria herself laid the foundation stone as work commenced in 1867, and she named the building after her late husband, Prince Albert, who had died six years earlier.

It was built in the highly popular Italianate style of architecture, and utilised cutting edge technology of the time to make the world's first domed amphitheatre. A freestanding structure constructed from glass and iron, the dome weighs an incredible 800 tons.

The hall was designed by civil engineers, Francis Fowke and Henry Y. D. Scott of the Royal Engineers, and built by the Lucas Brothers, who took inspiration from the amphitheatres of ancient Rome.

Constructed mainly from Fareham Red brick, the hall features a mosaic

The Royal Albert Hall.

Inside the Royal Albert Hall.

frieze which surrounds the building and measures 800 feet, comprising foot-long slabs of mosaic tiles illustrating the 'Triumph of the Arts and Sciences', with historical and religious quotations in terracotta above.

The glass and wrought-iron dome was built by the Manchester-based Fairbairn Engineering Company. The company assembled the dome on their own roof to ensure the 338 tonne iron metal frame could support the 279 tonne weight of glazing. After a successful trial, the dome was disassembled and transported to London on horse and cart.

The iron girders were attached to the roof's central elliptical ring one-by-one. The props that supported the dome were kicked away, and the dome dropped just 0.8 mm before settling into position on its supporting walls. The Hall was officially opened on 29 March 1871.

Decorative facade of the Royal Albert Hall.

Prolific Victorians

Trains

In the nineteenth century there was a big push to build London's great railways and associated terminals – St. Pancras, Liverpool Street, Paddington, King's Cross and Victoria stations were all built during this time. London Paddington set the standard – it was designed by the great Victorian engineer, Isambard Kingdom Brunel, and completed in 1854.

At the same time, planners wanted to solve the problem of traffic chaos within the city, and the answer was to move the networks underground. In 1863, the world's first underground railway was built, connecting Paddington station to Farringdon Street, providing wealthy commuters an easy journey to the Bank of England.

London Paddington, circa 1905.

St Pancras, 1908.

The first train on the Underground, 10 January 1863.

Leadenhall Market.

Leadenhall Market

While the market dates from the fourteenth century, the highly ornate green, burgundy and cream roof structure and cobbled floors of the current site were designed by Sir Horace Jones in 1881. Jones was also the architect behind Billingsgate and Smithfield Markets.

Natural History Museum

The natural history collections were originally set in the British Museum, but more space was needed and a separate building was planned.

The new building would be in South Kensington, and after the land was purchased, a competition was held to design the new museum in 1864. Captain Francis Fowke, a civil engineer, won with his design, but died soon after, and architect Alfred Waterhouse took over, revising the plans significantly and adding his own Romanesque style to the facades.

Work began in 1873 and the new museum opened in 1881. Terracotta was used for the entire building as this material was more resistant to Victorian London's harsh climate. The building is one of the UK's most impressive examples of Romanesque architecture, and has become a popular and iconic landmark.

Sewers

The Victorian era presided over enormous changes, including the construction of something that would drastically change the lives of London's population – sewers.

Before the sewer system was built, raw sewage went directly into the Thames. The Thames was also the source of drinking water for residents and consequently cholera was a big problem, with an epidemic killing around 10,000 people in 1853.

The government took action and commissioned engineer Joseph Bazalgette to design an underground network of sewers. Work started in 1859 and was virtually complete by 1868 at a cost of £4.2 million. The result was 82 miles of intercepting sewers running parallel to the River Thames, along with 1,100 miles of street sewers – a triumph of Victorian engineering.

The Natural History Museum.

Skeleton of a blue whale in the main hall of the Natural History Museum.

THE EDWARDIANS

At the advent of the twentieth century there was a sharp change in architectural taste. Neoclassicism was back in fashion, and now fused with the new styles of Beaux-Arts and Edwardian Baroque. With new materials at hand and grand plans, the city was to be transformed again...

The Edwardian era, during the brief reign of King Edward VII from 1901 to 1910, was a period thought to be the British equivalent of the French Belle Époque – full of optimism, peace, prosperity and innovation.

Edward VII was highly taken with the art and fashions of continental Europe, and this is seen in the fashion and architectural style of the time, with neoclassicism mixed with new Parisian styles.

Kingsway

With London's new found importance and wealth, many felt there was a need for a grand parade route through the capital of the kind often found in various European cities, and so the idea for Kingsway was born – a 30-metre-wide boulevard with an underground tram tunnel that would stretch all the way from the Strand to High Holborn.

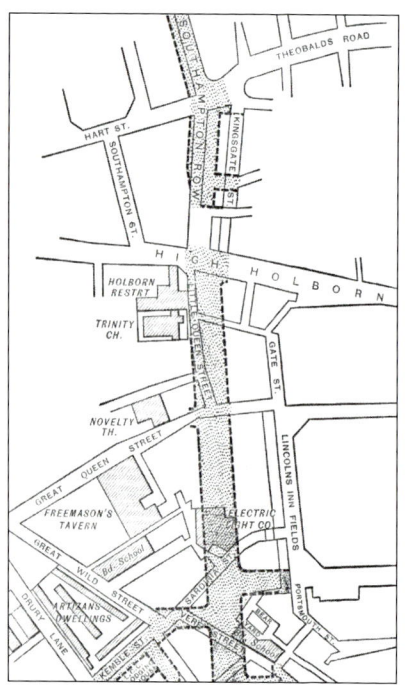

Map of Holborn, circa 1900, showing the route of Kingsway. Wikicommons

The Strand Improvement Bill of 1899 initiated the regeneration project and began a slum clearance programme that would see Clare Market, the notorious slum in Holborn which was set between Covent Garden and Lincoln's Inn Fields, completely removed.

Buildings were destroyed, including those dating back to the Elizabethan period that had survived the Great Fire of London.

Kingsway and Aldwych were built in their place. Aldwych formed a crescent-shaped road that connected the Strand to Kingsway. As the north of the Strand was torn down, it made way for a grand new boulevard lined with impressive new theatres, hotels and diplomatic buildings built in a Neoclassical style and clad in Portland stone, such as the headquarters of Britain's colonies, India House and Australia House. South Africa House was built opposite Trafalgar Square later in the 1930s.

The planners wanted to demolish two churches along the Strand that extended into the street and caused traffic issues, St Mary le Strand and the Wren-designed St Clement Danes, but there was such a public outcry that the Strand was instead widened to go around these churches, which created islands in the centre.

A group of buildings between The Mall and Trafalgar Square were torn down and replaced with the Neo-Baroque Admiralty Arch, which formed the grand east to west parade route encompassing Buckingham Palace, Trafalgar Square via Admiralty Arch, then connecting with the newly widened Strand to Fleet Street.

And so the impressive Kingsway was created, as well as the enormous processional route which stretches all the way from Buckingham Palace to St Paul's Cathedral.

The 25 metre high Victoria Memorial was placed in front of Buckingham Palace and unveiled in 1911. The memorial was encircled by four gates dedicated to the British dominions – Canada Gate, Australia Gate, as well as South and West Africa Gates.

Edwardian Architecture

The architectural fashion was now to echo the past, bringing elements of English Baroque from buildings such as Wren's St Paul's Cathedral and Jones's Banqueting House into modern designs.

Neo-Baroque was very much *en vogue* and the style was adopted in many of the government and religious buildings of this period, including the Old Bailey, County Hall and the War Office.

Some of the most fêted buildings in London were built during the Edwardian period, such as the Ritz Hotel on Piccadilly, Norman Shaw's Piccadilly Hotel and Selfridges department store, which were constructed in variations on the Neoclassic style, whether it was Beaux-Arts, Neo-Baroque or Louis XVI.

Steel

At the beginning of the twentieth century, steel was used more and more in construction to reinforce new buildings. Steel piers were used in isolation to support the rebuilt Harrods department store, while the Ritz Hotel was the first building in London to use steel framing for the whole construction, in 1906.

The new advances in engineering and steel production meant that domes were more straightforward to construct, and therefore proliferated during the Edwardian era. Steel girders made large domes lighter, cheaper to build, and much easier to engineer.

Selfridges on Oxford Street, which was modelled after American-style department stores, pushed the boundaries as far as steel-framed buildings were concerned. It was bigger than anything seen before in the capital and exceeded existing building regulations.

After plans for this were ushered through and the construction was a

Harrods.

success, steel reinforcement was the new standard for any large building in the city, and new developments along Aldwych and Kingsway all followed this new norm.

The Old Bailey

The Central Criminal Court of England and Wales, known as the Old Bailey after the street on which it stands, is one of a handful of buildings that house the Crown Court, and a prime example of the Neo-Baroque style.

In 1834, the Central Criminal Court Act established the Old Bailey as the principal court for London and the South East circuit. In 1902 the old sessions house and Newgate Prison were demolished to make way for the

The Old Bailey.

current building, which was opened in 1907 by King Edward VII.

The building was designed by E. W. Mountford and above the main entrance is inscribed: 'Defend the Children of the Poor & Punish the Wrongdoer'. On the dome above the court stands the court's symbolic gilt bronze statue of Lady Justice by sculptor F. W. Pomeroy from 1905. The statue holds a sword in the right hand and the scales of justice in the left. A remnant of the city wall is preserved in the basement beneath the cells.

Ritz Hotel

A Grade II listed 5-star hotel set in the heart of Piccadilly, the Ritz Hotel is one of the world's most prestigious hotels and synonymous with high society and luxury. Since its inception, the Ritz became so connected with luxury that the word 'ritzy' entered the English language to mean something fancy.

The brainchild of Swiss hotelier César Ritz and designed by the firm of Mewès & Davis, partners who were alumni of the École des Beaux-Arts and specialised in eighteenth century French architecture, the hotel opened in May 1906, eight years after he had established the Hôtel Ritz Paris.

After a slow start, the hotel gained popularity towards the end of the First World War, and became a hotspot

The Ritz Hotel circa 1910.

for socialites, writers, actors and politicians of the day, with people such as Noël Coward frequenting the Ritz in the 1920s and 1930s.

The building was created in the Neoclassical style, heavily influenced by the architectural fashions of Paris, and intended to resemble a Parisian block of flats set over shops, reminiscent of the Rue de Rivoli. At the corners of the pavilion roofs sit large green copper lions, the emblems of the hotel.

The Ritz was one of the earliest steel frame structures in London, following on from the Flatiron Building in New York City. Now because of the strong structure, the windows could be larger, any columns could be purely decorative, and larger areas such as the restaurant and Grand Gallery could be clear, open spaces.

César Ritz wanted the furniture, china and silver to be as fine as his guests had at home. Guests were even provided with silver curling tongs and glove stretchers, a telephone in every room, as well as a pneumatic tube for sending one's calling card to another guest in the hotel. It was an enormous success.

During the 1920s and '30s the hotel was more like a club – Nancy Mitford said it was 'a party where you see everybody you've ever known.' The hotel's steel structure was known

The Ritz Hotel today.

to be so sound that during the war the rich and famous left their own houses and moved in.

Selfridges

The Grade II listed Selfridges on Oxford Street, one of the most extravagant department stores in the world, opened towards the end of the Edwardian period in 1909, and is a rare example of the French Beaux-Arts movement in London.

It was in 1906 that American Harry Gordon Selfridge visited England with his wife, Rose, but found the British shops lacking – in his opinion they were lagging far behind their US counterparts.

Selfridge decided to build his own department store, investing £400,000 in the western, and at that time unfashionable, end of Oxford Street. He bought up a row of Georgian buildings to form his site.

The building was designed by American architect Daniel Burnham, who had previously designed department stores in the US, such as Marshall Field's in Chicago, and Gimbels and Wanamaker's in New York.

Incorporating the use of a steel frame, which was five stories high with three basement levels and a roof terrace, the building was originally laid out to accommodate 100 departments. The Swedish structural engineer Sven Bylander designed the steel frame structure, but had to jump many hurdles regarding building regulations, as the building was one of the very early examples of steel frame in the UK, which required making amendments to the London Building Act 1844.

Selfridges.

American architect Francis Swales designed the main face of the building with Ionic columns obscuring the view of the supporting steel columns, creating a uniform and classical Beaux-Arts facade.

The windows on the sides facing Oxford Street and Duke Street were constructed from cast iron frames to a size of 5.89 metres by 3.66 metres, so that the frontages comprise more glass than stone or iron. These are used to full effect to produce spectacular displays for which the store is well known.

The final design of the building was completed in 1928, and for many was the last great classical building constructed in the UK.

Sign, Oxford Street.

Tiles

During this period, glazed ceramic tiles were favoured over terracotta to clad buildings as they were easier to clean, which was a huge benefit in London's polluted atmosphere. This is seen in the London Underground stations built during the Edwardian years, such as those along the Piccadilly Line and Bakerloo Line.

Oxblood red tiles on the exterior of an obsolete station.

Green and white tiles inside a station.

ART DECO

After the 1925 World's Fair in Paris, the new Art Deco style exploded on to the scene in London, bringing clean lines, modern materials and flamboyant details into architecture, which feature in buildings such as the BBC Broadcasting House, the Daily Express Building and the Carreras Cigarette Factory in Mornington Crescent.

As the First World War finished, the mood was sombre in the war-damaged and cash-strapped Britain. Architects no longer turned to the opulence of the Neo-Baroque style and instead favoured the more simplistic and restrained stylings of Georgian times.

While Neo-Georgian was the style preferred for government architecture from around this time up until the 1960s, alongside this a new form of architecture began to emerge in 1925.

The 1925 International Exhibition of Modern Decorative and Industrial Arts in Paris was a World's Fair designed by the French government to showcase the new 'style moderne', later known as 'Art Deco'. It was here that new, avant-garde ideas in architecture and other arts were displayed for the very first time.

The Expo had a dramatic effect and Art Deco became a popular new form of architecture in London, as well as New York and Paris. The signature of the Art Deco style – clean lines, curves and bold colours, as well as the geometric patterns and elaborate sculptural features – were soon seen across some of the biggest cities in the world.

The clean lines of Art Deco were particularly popular with modern

1925 International Exhibition of Modern Decorative and Industrial Arts in Paris. Wikicommons

businesses such as the media, airports, cinemas, swimming pools and factories. The luxurious features of the style also appealed to hotels and theatres, as well as cutting-edge apartment blocks.

Media Architecture

On Fleet Street are two of the best examples of Art Deco architecture in London – the Daily Telegraph and the Daily Express buildings.

The facade of the Daily Express building is composed entirely of glass, vitrolite and chromium. The modern materials cut an aesthetic which stood out sharply against the

The Daily Express building circa 1978. Wikicommons

The Art Deco home of the **Daily Express** *newspaper.* Wikicommons

The Daily Telegraph building.

BBC Broadcasting House.

other brick and stone buildings that lined Fleet Street. While industrial, sleek materials like this were common in the Art Deco buildings seen in New York, they were unusual in London, where Portland stone was still the favoured material.

The Daily Telegraph building was constructed from the more traditional material of Portland stone, but incorporated Egyptian decorations and an impressive colonnade facade in a nod to the Art Deco style.

Another fine example of Art Deco architecture is the BBC's Broadcasting House set on Portland Place, constructed again from Portland stone, but decorated with sculptures created by Eric Gill.

Carreras Cigarette Factory

The Carreras Cigarette Factory in Mornington Crescent, Camden, was an unusual creation, combining Art Deco with Egyptian motifs.

The building was constructed between 1926 and 1928 by the Carreras Tobacco Company, owned by the Russian-Jewish inventor and philanthropist Bernhard Baron.

Greater London House, previously the Carreras Cigarette Factory. Wikicommons

During the First World War, demand grew for cigarettes and business was booming for the tobacco company. By the 1920s, they needed to expand and Carreras moved from its Arcadia cigarette factory in City Road, London, and opened a new Arcadia Works in Mornington Crescent in 1928.

The design was highly influenced by the fashion of the time for Egyptian-style buildings, and came four years after the 1922 expedition which uncovered the tomb of Tutankhamun. This captured the imagination of many writers, artists and architects, who were also inspired by the Egyptian Art Deco themes in the Paris Exhibition of 1925.

The Carreras Cigarette Factory's distinctive Egyptian-style ornamentation originally included a solar disc to the Sun-god Ra, two gigantic effigies of black cats (stylised versions of the Egyptian god Bastet) flanking the entrance and colourful painted details, with the building designed as a temple to 'Bastet'. The building was faced in Atlas White cement, which was coloured to look like sand.

The front of the building was lined with 12 papyriform columns, painted in bright colours with Venetian glass decoration, thought to have been inspired by columns at tombs in Amarna. The handrails on the staircase to the main entrance were in the shape of serpents, while the railings around the building featured Egyptian hieroglyphs.

The factory was opened with great ceremony with an event in front of the building. The pavements were covered in sand to replicate the deserts of Egypt, and there was a procession of cast members from a production of Verdi's opera *Aida*, where actors in Ancient Egyptian costume performed around the 'temple' structure. This was followed by a chariot race on Hampstead Road.

The factory was converted into offices in 1961 and much of the Egyptian detailing was stripped from the building, but it was carefully restored during an extensive renovation in the late 1990s, with replicas of the famous cats placed outside the entrance.

Senate House

Set in the heart of Bloomsbury, Senate House was designed by Charles Holden to be the new base for the University of London, which was in urgent need of new office and teaching space.

Constructed between 1932 and 1937, the building comprises 19 storeys and reached 64 metres tall. The imposing Art Deco building was one of the very first skyscrapers in Britain, and is the tallest Art Deco building in the capital.

Senate House was criticised at the time of its construction for standing out so much from the rather modest Georgian squares of Bloomsbury. Evelyn Waugh even went as far as to describe it as 'the vast bulk of London University insulting the autumnal sky'.

The building was used during the Second World War as the Ministry of Information, which served as inspiration for George Orwell's Ministry of Truth in his novel *Nineteen Eighty-Four*.

Ironically, there was also a rumour that Hitler wanted his London headquarters to be based at Senate House after he had conquered Britain, and had ordered bombers to avoid it during the Blitz.

Two effigies of black cats flank the entrance to the former Carreras Cigarette Factory. Wikicommons

Senate House.

Simpsons of Piccadilly

A retail store, Simpsons of Piccadilly was created by Alexander Simpson and architect Joseph Emberton. It opened in April 1936 and was the largest menswear store in Britain at the time. It is now a Grade I listed building due to its innovative construction.

When Simpson bought the site, his aim was to build a large, modern store to serve as a flagship for the Simpson brand. He wanted a store with a strong steel structure, faced in the ever popular Portland stone, to be built as high as possible to compete with the store built for the rival Austin Reed ten years previously.

What resulted was a structure regarded as Joseph Emberton's masterpiece. Large sections of Portland stone alternating with strips of windows span the width of the building, and he incorporated a glass wall that stretched the height of the store at over 27 metres, which lit each open-plan floor with natural light. An impressive Travertine marble staircase spiralled up the middle of the building, and the store included the first curved-glass windows in Britain.

Simpson was unusual in that he wanted the building elements that were typically hidden to be on display and to show their function. The smaller details were also important, and Simpson had Emberton design the shop fittings and lighting, such as the 90-foot chromium light fitting suspended from the ceiling of the staircase, as well as the steel and

Simpsons of Piccadilly. Wikicommons

glass handrails. On the fifth floor there was also a balcony that allowed views across London to Westminster Abbey and St Paul's Cathedral.

A director of the Bauhaus school, László Moholy-Nagy, was responsible for designing the displays for the shop, including the in-store signage, and even arranged for three aircraft to be exhibited on the fifth floor at the store opening to draw in the crowds.

Lighting in Simpsons of Piccadilly. Wikicommons

Simpson also included other services in the store such as a gift shop, a dog shop, a barber's and a restaurant.

The building was made to such a high specification as dictated by Simpson that the costs spiralled and the company did not expect to make a profit for several years after the construction, but the results of their efforts were incredibly modern and it was a triumph.

Simpson continued to trade in the Piccadilly store until the 1990s. The building was later purchased by the Waterstones chain of bookshops, and currently serves as their flagship store.

Art Deco department store. Wikicommons

Battersea Power Station

Battersea Power Station is one of Britain's most famous buildings, and sits on London's most prominent riverside location.

During the 1920s, private companies would construct small power stations which would supply electricity for individual industries, giving any surplus energy to the public supply. Naturally, this created a rather chaotic system, which led parliament to decree that electricity would be set in a single system and kept under the ownership of the public, and so the London Power Company was formed in 1925.

The construction of the first super power station followed soon after, and the site chosen was Battersea. The building was designed by Sir Giles Gilbert Scott, who also designed the iconic red telephone box. Architect J. Theo Halliday collaborated with Scott on the project.

The new structure would be a coal-fired power station with a steel girder frame and exterior brick cladding. Construction of Station A began in 1929, while Station B started later and did not become operational until 1953. All four of the chimneys were completed by 1955 – these behemoths were constructed from concrete and stood 103 metres tall. Both of the connected stations consisted of a long boiler house with a chimney at each

Battersea Power Station.

end and an adjacent turbine hall. The station also included jetty facilities for unloading coal, a coal sorting and storage area, control rooms and an administration block. The power station became the largest brick building in Europe.

Halliday gave the control room of Station A Art Deco fittings, and Italian marble was used in the turbine hall, while wrought-iron staircases and polished parquet floors were used throughout. The interior of Station B however, was not so plush. Money was lacking after the Second World War, so there were fewer Art Deco flourishes, and the fittings were made from stainless steel.

The design of the station was an enormous hit, described as a 'temple of power', and in a 1939 survey by *The Architectural Review* it was ranked as the second favourite modern building by a panel of celebrities.

Decommissioning

In 1975, due to its output falling with age, Station A was closed after 40 years in operation, and by 1983 the power station had ceased to produce electricity altogether. As the building had been given Grade II status due to

Building work at Battersea Power Station.

the Art Deco features, the Electricity Board could not demolish the site and sell off the land as they had hoped.

The power station stood derelict as various ideas for redevelopment were presented. Finally, in 2013, construction began to transform the building into a community of over 800 homes, workspaces, shops and restaurants, with 18 acres of open space.

The plans also included the restoration of the structure of the power station, as well as the Art Deco features, the reconstruction of the chimneys and the refurbishment of the historic jetty and cranes.

Remaking the chimneys

The building's four iconic chimneys were rebuilt using the same techniques as the original construction. In May 2015, the first pour was carried out, and over the next two years, around 680 tonnes of concrete were hand-poured to form the 51 metre-tall chimneys, which were completed in June 2017.

To form the chimneys, a 'Jump Form' shuttering method was used. This technique involved steel and timber rings being filled with concrete before being moved up and then filled again. During the entire process, the hoist travelled the equivalent of 21 miles.

10

POST WAR DESIGN

After the Second World War, London was in desperate need of repair, and urban planners used this as an opportunity to redefine the area and create a better city. Modernist and Brutalist Architecture dominated with buildings such as the Royal Festival Hall, the Royal National Theatre and the Barbican.

London was ravaged in the Blitz, which resulted in almost 20,000 civilians killed and over a million houses destroyed or damaged. After most inhabitants had been evacuated to safer areas, rebuilding the city became a priority. With a spirit of post-war optimism, the government commissioned urban planner and professor of town planning at the University of London, Sir Patrick Abercrombie, to rebuild the capital and solve the housing crisis. He used this opportunity to redesign the capital with the County of London Plan.

Working with a team including London County Council's chief architect, J. H. Forshaw, they came up with a plan to create a better city, believing that this could be engineered on drawing boards and delivered from the top down.

They surveyed the current situation, the buildings, traffic and lifestyle of the inhabitants and drew reams of new designs. They wanted to make London the best it could be, to eradicate slums

Patrick Abercrombie. Wikicommons

and create green spaces in all areas of the city, rather than just in some privileged parts. They had already begun to clear out the condemned and obsolete houses in the years before the war, and wanted to take this further in their vision for the area.

The County of London Plan, produced in 1943, was the first of two ambitious documents for the post-war improvement of the capital. Together with the subsequent Greater London Plan of 1944 they became known collectively as the Abercrombie Plan.

The design depicted a green capital city providing space for its inhabitants to enjoy healthier living in what was considered a golden era for planning, and one that did not have to adhere to the many current requirements or public consultation.

The vision included people living together in communities, set around schools, with shops and wide open spaces for children to play, while people would work on trading estates. Wide tree-lined roads would connect communities, and factories and

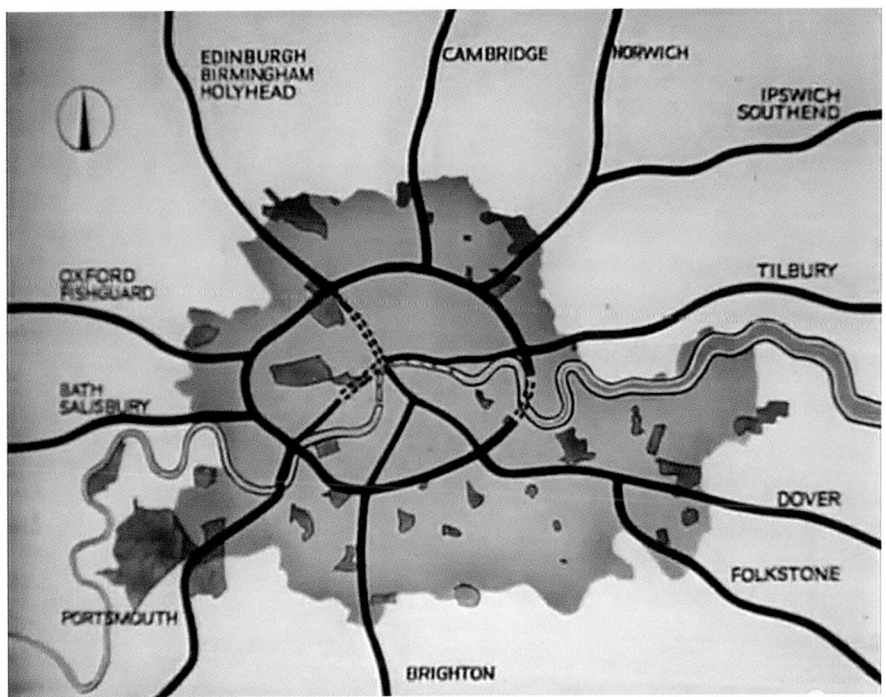

Section of the County of London Plan, 1945. Wikicommons

industrial buildings would be separated from residential areas.

Larger roads would be set around the communities, so that traffic would not be congested within the neighbourhoods. They planned for a ring road around London with two roads across the centre to separate faster roads from local roads.

The planners wanted to clear some of the south bank so that Londoners could appreciate the river. They said, 'On the south bank there is a confusion of warehouses, slums and derelict streets. Worse since the Blitz. Here is an opportunity to create a new riverfront worthy of its position in the heart of the capital.'

People were relocated to the suburbs to allow the inner city areas to be regenerated, leaving just over 5,000 local residents in the capital. During this time, residential areas such as the Golden Lane Estate and the Barbican were built, which are fine examples of urban reconstruction and became symbols of the post war recovery effort.

Many schools and public buildings were also built over the period, and The Greater London Plan contained most of the major physical developments

Housing block with yellow panels at Golden Lane Estate.

Golden Lane Estate.

that the capital has since seen, such as new towns, the M25 orbital motorway, Heathrow and Gatwick airports and the greenbelt of protected countryside which surrounds the city. Roads and industrial zones were separated from living areas.

The Southbank is a particular triumph, with many buildings of note appearing after the plan, including The Royal Festival Hall and the Royal National Theatre, two masterpieces in concrete.

The Royal Festival Hall

Set on the south bank of the River Thames, the Royal Festival Hall is a 2,700-seat concert venue within the Southbank Centre, home to the London Philharmonic Orchestra, and the first post-war building to become Grade I listed.

Built as part of the Festival of Britain for London County Council, the hall was officially opened on 3 May 1951. The chief architect for the project was Robert Matthew, who worked with designers such as Leslie Martin.

A sketch from 1948 by Martin shows the idea behind the design – the egg in a box. The auditorium is at the centre, with symmetrically placed staircases

The Royal Festival Hall.

and galleries surrounding it. The interior space was arranged with wide open foyers, and the staircase gave a sense of ceremony. The bars and restaurants were open to all, and as these spaces were built around the auditorium, they also insulated the hall from the noise of the nearby railway bridge.

The project was designed to be impressive and modern, eschewing the classicism of similar buildings. The hall was built in a Modernist style with reinforced concrete, and featured luxurious flourishes using beautiful woods and Derbyshire fossilised limestone. The exterior of the building was bright white with large areas of glass on the facade so that the interior was flooded with light.

Prime Minister Clement Attlee laid the foundation stone for the Royal Festival Hall in 1949. The building cost £2 million to construct, and opened in 1951 with a gala concert attended by King George VI and Queen Elizabeth.

The Festival Hall was taken over by the Arts Council in 1986, and managed together with the Queen Elizabeth Hall and Purcell Room, as well as the Hayward Gallery, eventually becoming an independent arts organisation now known as the Southbank Centre.

Royal National Theatre

The National Theatre is one of London's most famous Brutalist buildings, once described by Prince Charles as looking like 'a nuclear power station'.

The enormous building houses three theatres, as well as restaurants, bars, foyers, workshops and more. Designed by Denys Lasdun and completed in 1976, the building is also set on the south bank and comprises various strata of horizontal terraces with two towers on top.

Constructed from concrete, the design was intended by Lasdun to be 'architecture as urban landscape'. The layers of the building were planned to fuse with the south bank using strategies such as interconnected walkways, stairwells and split levels in order to blur where the theatre and the street end and begin.

Rough-cast concrete was used as the surface of the theatre, both inside and out, and the walls still have the imprints of the timber planks used to form the structure. Lasdun said, 'Concrete is a very intractable material, but it can be a beautiful material if it is used in the way its own nature intends it to be used... It is a sort of sculpture that you can only do with reinforced concrete, but you need to work to a certain scale... It is not a cosy little material.'

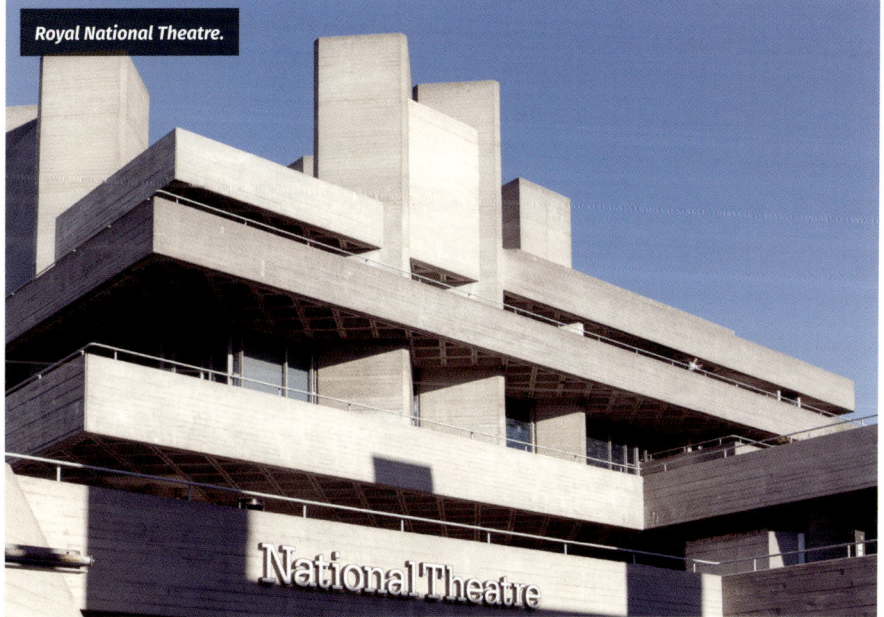

Royal National Theatre.

Just 18 years after completion, the building was given Grade II listing status, and is a prime example of modern architecture in London today.

Barbican

A project of enormous size and complexity, the Barbican redevelopment scheme took nearly three decades to design and build.

The design comprised more than 2,000 flats and two schools, as well as an arts centre. To build the structure, it was first necessary to realign an Underground tube line and excavate 190,000 cubic metres of soil. At the peak of the construction, over 1,000 workers were employed on the project.

Now considered one of the most important modernist architectural firms in post-war England, Chamberlin, Powell & Bon designed the Barbican Estate. The architects created three different plans for the area between 1955 and 1959. Initially suggesting a small exhibition hall in the first draft, by 1959 this had transformed into a major arts centre complete with theatre, concert hall, art gallery and library, as well as a restaurant.

Construction began in 1963, and took 12 years to complete. The facade consists of tooled concrete, which was

View of the Barbican Estate.

Barbican Estate.

an incredibly laborious technique. When the concrete had set, the surface was tooled with great precision, using handheld pick hammers to uncover the coarse granite aggregate underneath.

The architects and engineers used clever techniques to squeeze in the enormous new arts centre. They dug down 20 metres, and set the majority of the centre below ground, comparing the centre to 'the hull of a large ship in which much is contained below the water.'

The Barbican Complex exemplifies British brutalist architecture and is now Grade II listed.

The iconic brutalist-style architecture of the Barbican.

CONTEMPORARY ARCHITECTURE

The 1970s brought postmodernism and high tech to architecture in London with new designs in the form of the MI6 Building and The Lloyd's Building. One of the most famous architects, Norman Foster, rose to prominence in the 1990s with work such as The Gherkin.

The late 1970s brought great stylistic change to construction in London. A turning point in the history of architecture, the postmodern movement began in a reaction against the more formal and solemn modernism which had heavily influenced architectural design in the post-war years.

A movement that rejected minimalism, post-modern architecture instead welcomed a sense of playfulness and irony, and often referenced pop culture, as well as historical styles. These influences resulted in wildly eccentric buildings which contrasted sharply with the post war modernism and Brutalist architecture.

SIS Building

Perhaps London's best-known example of postmodernist architecture is Terry Farrell's SIS Building, the headquarters of the British Secret Intelligence Service.

Set along the Albert Embankment area of the River Thames next to Vauxhall Bridge, the SIS Building has an extremely distinctive pyramidal style which was influenced by Mayan and Aztec temple design.

Completed in 1994, the building is, ironically for a secret service headquarters, one of London's most famous structures. The headquarters of the organisation had previously been set in an office block near Waterloo Station, but had been beset with security issues.

Prime Minister Margaret Thatcher agreed to the new building in 1988, and the Albert Embankment site was purchased for £135.05 million, with a

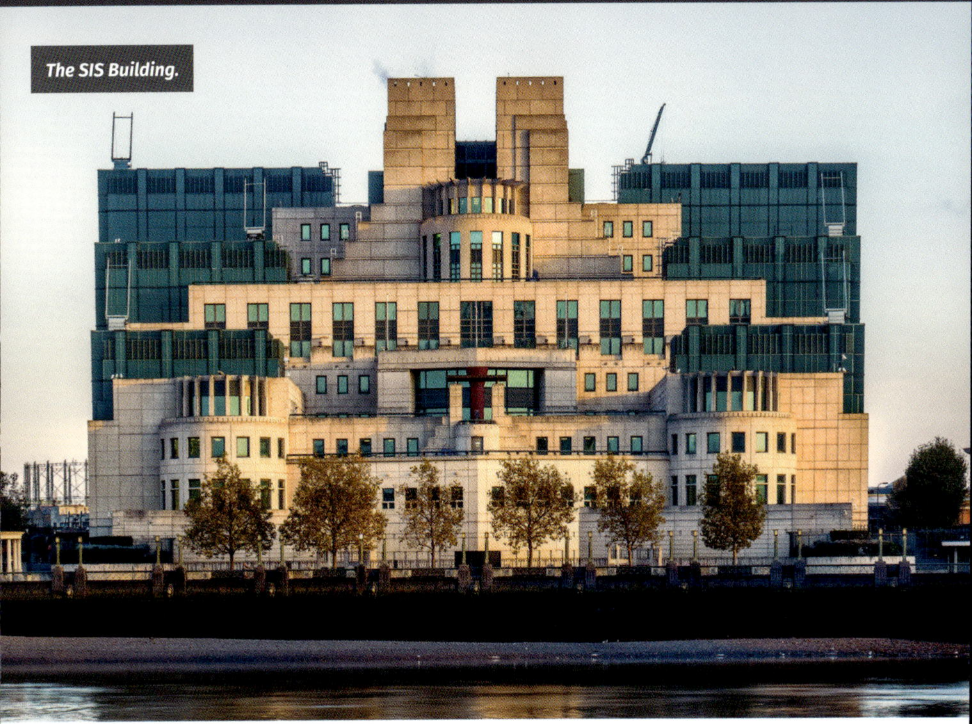

The SIS Building.

The SIS Building and St George Wharf buildings and tower.

further £152.6 million budgeted for the building itself.

The building incorporated a great number of high tech defensive features, including bomb blast protection and emergency back-up systems, as well as triple-glazed windows constructed from 25 different types of glass.

Layered blocks were built up to create the ancient temple design, which gave the building 60 separate roof areas. The SIS building also extends underground below street level, and features a protective moat. Rumour has it there is a tunnel that leads to Whitehall travelling underneath the Thames.

Officially opened by Queen Elizabeth II in July 1994, the building has since featured in many of the James Bond films, including *The World Is Not Enough* from 1999 and then again in *Spectre* from 2015.

British Library

The British Library is the UK's national library and with over 150 million items it is the second largest in the world. Located at St Pancras, and extending deep underground, construction work

The British Library.

The British Library sign.

began in 1962 and was completed in 1997, finally opening to the public in 1998.

The red brick library, with a large courtyard filled with sculptures, was derided as an eyesore and waste of money by several politicians and commentators, including Prince Charles. Indeed, it was described as being 'one of the ugliest buildings in the world' by a parliamentary committee.

However, in recent years The British Library has undergone something of a reappraisal and was awarded Grade I listing status in 2015 in recognition of its 'outstanding architectural and historic interest'.

Statue to the front of the British Library.

Lloyd's of London

A part of the postmodern movement that started to become prominent in the late twentieth century was the high tech and Neo-futurist style, which fused the eccentricity and unusual shapes of the postmodern wave with the functionality of the modernist movement. These styles used glass, steel and high-tech processes, and often exposed the structures within as decoration.

Nowhere is this seen more keenly than in the Lloyd's Building, a spectacular example from 1986 by Richard Rogers, located at 1 Lime Street in the City of London. The building incorporates an 'inside-out' design where the utilities, lifts and pipes are all placed on the outside and become the facade, the decoration itself, as opposed to being concealed and taking up space inside the building.

Home to insurance market Lloyd's of London, the building is one of the most iconic in the capital, and a leading example of the high-tech architectural style, combining both industrial and futuristic features.

Lloyd's of London had been on nearby Leadenhall Street since 1928, but needed to expand 30 years later and moved to Lime Street. A need

Lloyd's of London.

The 'inside-out' design of Lloyd's of London.

for further expansion in the 1970s necessitated another move and the current site was purchased.

Lloyd's commissioned Richard Rogers to design a building they could use well into the next century, one with flexible space that would be able to accommodate their changing requirements, but also a building where they could continue to work during the construction, which would involve the current building from 1928 being demolished.

The plan was revolutionary. Richard Rogers created a design where the main underwriting room in the building could grow or shrink depending on the requirements of the time, using a series of galleries around the central area. Services were banished to the perimeter to maximise the space available to the underwriters.

During the construction, care was taken with the impact on surrounding buildings, particularly the listed nineteenth century Leadenhall Market.

It was a difficult process but the results were spectacular. The cutting edge building was officially opened in 1986 after a construction period of 8 years. It cost around £75 million

Lloyd's of London in autumn.

to build, stood 88 metres tall and contained 14 floors. The cranes were left on top of the building for further modification if necessary.

The building has three main towers, each with its own service tower, and a 60-metre high atrium sits in the centre, housing the main underwriting room. The room is naturally lit by a vaulted glass roof, which was inspired by Joseph Paxman's Crystal Palace, and features 12 glass lifts, the first to be seen in the UK.

As the services were located on the exterior, the interior of the building is flexible, as planned, with each floor easily altered by the addition or removal of partitions. Escalators zigzag across the central atrium to create a sense of circulation between the floors.

Although the building created a great deal of controversy due to the sharp contrast with the surroundings, it is now acknowledged to be one of the greatest architectural achievements of the 1980s and a true icon of London, balancing high tech efficiency with high concept architectural design. In 2011, it became the youngest building ever to receive Grade I listed status.

Lifts on the exterior of the Lloyd's of London building.

30 St Mary Axe

More commonly known as 'the Gherkin', 30 St Mary Axe is another spectacular example of high tech architecture. Housing commercial offices and set in the City of London, the building has become a London landmark since its completion in 2003.

The previous building to stand on the site was the Baltic Exchange. This was damaged in 1992, when the Provisional IRA exploded a bomb

The peak of the Gherkin.

30 St Mary Axe.

nearby which caused a huge amount of damage to the facade of the building and it was decided to replace it with a new development.

Norman Foster and Arup created an extraordinary design with a circular plan, widening in profile as it rises before tapering near the apex to give the building the famous 'gherkin' shape. However, although the building is curved, the only curved piece of glass lies in the cap at the very pinnacle.

There are several innovative features within the building. At the perimeter there are high tech diagonal braces which allow for more floor space inside the structure as there is no need for supporting columns. There are also gaps in each floor which act as a ventilation system – warm air is vented out during warm months and drawn in during the winter. Due to the efficient design the energy consumed by the building is around half that of a typical skyscraper.

The very top level on the 40th floor is home to a bar for tenants and their guests, while the 39th floor houses a restaurant, with private dining rooms on the floor below.

Construction began in 2001 and was completed two years later,

Geometric design of the Gherkin.

opening in April 2004. The Gherkin subsequently won that year's RIBA Stirling Prize in an unanimous decision by the judges.

In 2007, the building was sold to IVG Immobilien AG and UK investment firm Evans Randall for £630 million.

Just seven years later, the building was sold again for £700 million to the Safra Group.

30 St Mary Axe was a turning point in high rise architecture for the capital, and it wouldn't be long before many other buildings would follow suit...

Norman Foster

Born 1 June 1935 in Manchester, Norman Foster is one of the most significant and prolific British architects of the modern day. He is known for his sleek, modern buildings, and responsible for the Gherkin in London, Hearst Tower in New York, the Reichstag building redevelopment in Berlin and London City Hall, along with many, many more.

Norman Foster. Wikicommons

Richard Rogers

Richard George Rogers, born 23 July 1933, is an Italian-British architect, famous for his modernist designs and high tech architecture. His most significant buildings include the Pompidou Centre in Paris, which he designed along with Renzo Piano, the Lloyd's building, and the Millennium Dome in London. He has won a whole host of awards including the RIBA Gold Medal and the Pritzker Prize.

Richard Rogers. Wikicommons

TWENTY-FIRST CENTURY LONDON

Since the millennium, there has been a wave of incredible buildings, including the Shard, the Cheesegrater, the Tate Modern and the London Aquatics Centre, all continuing the legacy of original and revolutionary architecture in the capital.

The first skyscraper in the City of London was considered to be The NatWest Tower, now called Tower 42, completed in 1980, and standing at 183 metres. It was the tallest building in the UK at the time and also held the title of the tallest cantilever building in the world.

Just over ten years later, One Canada Square was completed as

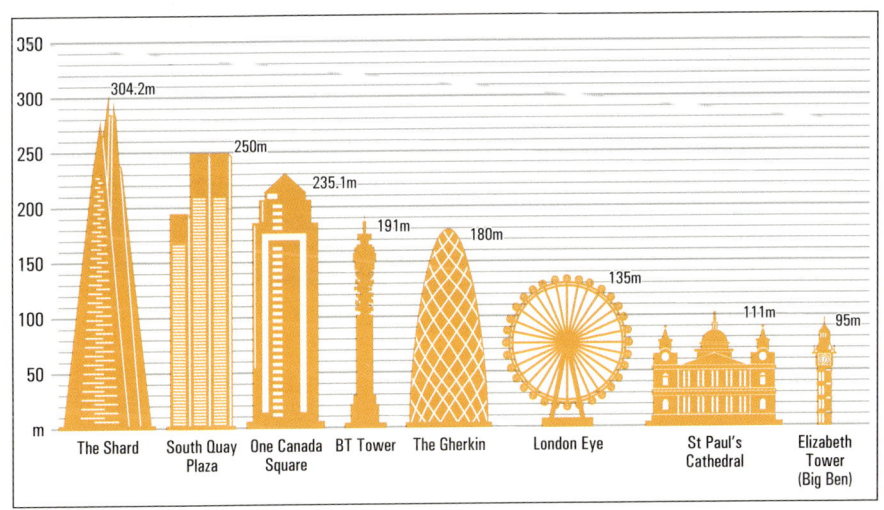

the centrepiece of the Canary Wharf development in 1991 which dwarfed The NatWest Tower, and stood at 235 metres, taking the title of the tallest building in the UK.

The new trend for high rise building was encouraged by the city planners and the Mayor of London at the time, Ken Livingstone. Over the next 10 years, two skyscrapers, 8 Canada Square and 25 Canada Square, each rose to an impressive 200 metres tall in Canary Wharf, completed in 2002.

Many more followed. In 2003, Canary Wharf added Heron Quays at 153 metres and 10 Upper Bank Street at 151 metres to its collection of skyscrapers, closely followed in 2004 with 25 Bank Street, standing at 153 metres.

At the same time in the City of London, 30 St Mary Axe was completed, 180 metres high, with Heron Tower following in 2007 at 230 metres, and the Broadgate Tower in 2008 at 165 metres.

Boris Johnson, Mayor of London from 2008 to 2016, approved the construction of more skyscrapers in London as the capital's skyline rose steadily higher.

The Scalpel, rising 190 metres, was completed in the City of London in 2018 and skyscrapers continue to be built in this part of London, as well as Canary Wharf and new areas such as Vauxhall and Nine Elms.

The Shard

Possibly the most iconic building in the city, the Shard, set next to London Bridge Station, pierces the London skyline at an incredible 309.6 metres tall. Completed in 2012, The Shard still stands as the tallest building in the UK today and is among the 100 tallest buildings in the world.

The developer and joint owner is Irvine Sellar, whose vision was to build a 'vertical city', comprising offices, apartments, shops, hotels and restaurants, as well as a public viewing gallery.

Sellar acquired Southwark Towers in 1998, and in 2000 architect Renzo Piano began designing the church spire-like structure that would appear to rise from the River Thames 'like a shard of glass'.

Various bodies were quick to object, including the Commission for Architecture and the Built Environment (CABE), and heritage bodies such as English Heritage (now Historic England), and a planning inquiry was launched in 2002.

Despite the objections, planning permission was granted and announced in 2003 by Deputy Prime Minister John Prescott.

The building company Mace was awarded the contract in 2007, agreeing a fixed price of £350 million, which increased to nearly £435 million by the following year. At this point, the world was in crisis and an economic

The Shard at sunset.

recession posed a major threat to the project. However, the State of Qatar stepped in and agreed to buy out the original stakeholders.

Design

Inspired by the geometry of the railway lines near the site, as well as London's church spires and the masts of sailing ships, Piano's tapered design uses a sophisticated form of glazing which features angled glass panes that reflect sunlight and the sky above.

The construction used a revolutionary technique in which the foundations were excavated using a top-down method that allowed the core of the first 23 storeys to be built upward simultaneously.

This was a pioneering and necessary step due to the construction of such a tall skyscraper in a hugely built-up area next to a major train station, and helped speed up the process so that the project was completed quickly.

There were many other firsts and various achievements during the course of the build, which included the largest concrete pour, the first use of jump-lift construction and the first inclined hoist in the world, as well as the first crane to be supported on a slipform.

The frame of the Shard is a mix of composite steel, post-tension concrete, traditional reinforced concrete and pre-fabricated steel. The iconic building is clad with 11,000 panes of glass, with a total surface area of 56,000 square metres.

An opening ceremony was held on 5 July 2012 by the Prime Minister of Qatar, which featured a flamboyant laser show.

As planned, the skyscraper works as a vertical city, with 13 floors of apartments, a 17-storey hotel, three floors of restaurants, and 25 floors of office space, as well as spectacular viewing galleries on the 69th and the 72nd floor.

The Shard.

The Cheesegrater

The Leadenhall Building at 122 Leadenhall Street, known as 'the Cheesegrater' due to its distinctive slanting profile, was designed by architects Rogers Stirk Harbour + Partners and developed by British Land and Oxford Properties.

The iconic design stems from the planning stipulation that the structure should not obscure views of St Paul's Cathedral, hence the tapered shape.

The high tech 225 metre tall tower has 48 floors and a glass facade with an innovative structure underneath.

A concrete core is usually used to provide the strength and stability for a building of this height, but the Cheesegrater instead has the world's tallest megaframe constructed from steel to provide stability, which includes an enormous ladder frame with steel bracings criss-crossing the structure.

The Shard set along the South Bank.

The Leadenhall Building.

Skyscrapers in the City.

High rise London.

The flat side of the building is clad in glass and houses the mechanical services, such as the elevator shafts, which have become an architectural feature similar to those in the nearby Lloyd's building. At the base is an atrium with ceilings 30 metres high, which is open to the public.

Construction of the basement floors began in 2011, and the building was officially opened by the Duke of Cambridge and Prince Harry on 19 October 2015.

In June 2018, the Leadenhall Building was announced as a RIBA National Award winner, with the judges saying the building was 'one of the more striking and elegant towers to have been added to the City's jumbled skyline in recent years. Its theatrical backside ensure that all lifts and toilets are choreographed into a circulation and servicing core at the rear, again glazed. This creates a constant intricate dance of lifts of different colours and sizes and their inhabitants, rising and falling, filling and emptying. Functional necessity becomes something beautiful to watch – almost like a children's storybook of How a Building Works...'

Tate Modern

Set in the former Bankside Power Station on the south bank of the Thames, the Tate Modern is one of the most famous and iconic contemporary art galleries in the world.

The Tate Modern.

The Tate Modern Turbine Hall.

Tate Modern Switch House.

The power station was originally designed by Sir Giles Gilbert Scott, the architect who created Battersea Power Station, and was constructed between 1947 and 1963, as a 200 metre long, steel-framed, brick-clad building.

The power station closed in 1981 and developers clambered to redevelop the iconic structure. Herzog & de Meuron were awarded the commission in 1995 to redevelop the building as an art gallery and the highly ambitious £134 million project was completed in 2000.

In 2016, the Switch House, a 10 storey, 65 metre high extension, was added, which included a new 360-degree viewing gallery. Again designed by Herzog & de Meuron, the extension added 60 percent more space to be used for live art, installations and film. It has been touted as Britain's most important new cultural building for almost two decades.

The Switch House building is a pyramid-like structure with the brickwork in a lattice form, while the interior is made from exposed concrete. A public terrace on the top floor offers panoramic views of London, and a new bridge spanning the Turbine Hall joins the existing galleries in the Boiler House with the new galleries in the Switch House.

With sustainability high on the agenda and various eco features such as natural ventilation, solar panels and green spaces, the Mayor of London Sadiq Khan, described the Tate as 'a modern museum for the twenty-first century'.

The brick pattern of the Switch House.

London Aquatics Centre

The spectacular London Aquatics Centre set in the Queen Elizabeth Olympic Park, Stratford, is an indoor swimming centre and one of the main venues created for the 2012 Summer Olympics and Paralympics. The centre comprises two 50-metre swimming pools and a 25-metre diving pool. Designed by Zaha Hadid in 2004, the structure was inspired by the fluidity of water seen in the stunning undulating roof.

London Aquatics Centre.

Renzo Piano

Born into a family of builders on 14 September 1937, Renzo Piano is an Italian architect who, along with Richard Rogers, designed the ultra high tech Centre Georges Pompidou in Paris, which redefined what a museum should be. He also created the iconic Shard in London, as well as the Whitney Museum of American Art in New York, and won the Pritzker Architecture Prize in 1998.

Renzo Piano. Wikicommons

Zaha Hadid

Born 31 October 1950, Zaha Hadid was a British Iraqi architect, as well as an artist and designer. Some of her major works include the London Aquatics Centre for the 2012 Olympics, the Guangzhou Opera House and the Broad Art Museum in Michigan. She was described by *The Guardian* as the 'Queen of the curve', and was the first woman to receive the Pritzker Architecture Prize in 2004.

Zaha Hadid. Wikicommons

INDEX